WING CHUN
KUNG FU
THE WOODEN DUMMY

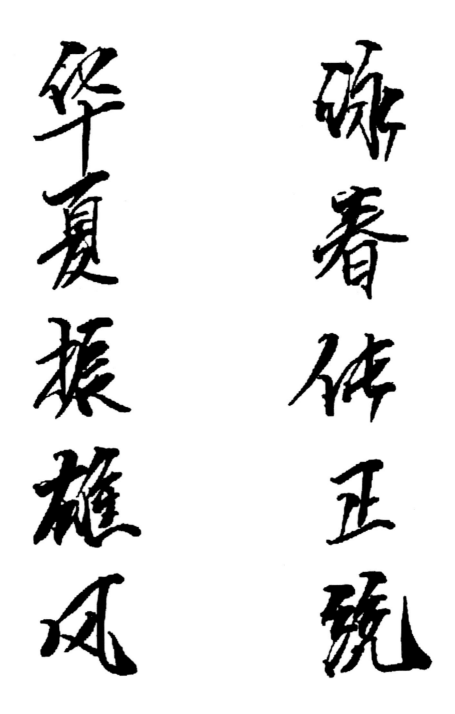

Fig 1   Wing Chun passing down the traditional way, making the whole nation stronger.

WING CHUN KUNG FU
THE WOODEN DUMMY

Sifu Shaun Rawcliffe

Forewords by Sifu Garry McKenzie and Paul S. Clifton

THE CROWOOD PRESS

First published in 2008 by
The Crowood Press Ltd
Ramsbury, Marlborough
Wiltshire SN8 2HR

www.crowood.com

This impression 2017

British Library Cataloguing-in-Publication Data
A catalogue record for this book is available from the British Library.

ISBN 978 1 84797 026 8

Disclaimer
Please note that the author and the publisher of this book are not
responsible in any manner whatsoever for any damage or injury of any
kind that may result from practising, or applying, the principles, ideas,
techniques and/or following the instructions/information described in
this publication. Since the physical activities described in this book may
be too strenuous in nature for some readers to engage in safely, it is
essential that a doctor be consulted before undertaking training.

Dedication
To my beautiful wife Genea and my fabulous daughter Kennedy.

Typeset in Plantin by Bookcraft Ltd, Stroud, Gloucestershire
Printed and bound in Malaysia by Times Offset (M) Sdn Bhd

Contents

Forewords

Before expressing my thoughts on this book, I feel it necessary to give a little background on how I came to know Shaun, a friend, a brother and a fellow martial artist. Although we come from the same Wing Chun root, I met Shaun in 1992 when I had the opportunity to arrange a seminar for Bruce Lee's student James De Mille. At that time, I was in the Wing Chun wilderness, and I had started to learn Cantonese with the intention of visiting Hong Kong in search of a Sifu, which I found in Grandmaster Ip Ching. We connected instantly and I have Shaun and Samuel Kwok to thank for that all-important introduction. They both advised me on the protocol of how to navigate myself around the Hong Kong Wing Chun circuit.

This book is timely in that many practitioners are now learning or have learnt the Muk Yan Jong techniques. To the untrained eye, the way in which many individuals play the Muk Yan Jong may seem impressive. For example, I remember when Jackie Chan's movie *Rumble in the Bronx* was released, and everyone witnessed him display some manoeuvres on the Muk Yan Jong at lightning speed. I recall one experienced Wing Chun Sifu saying, 'Wow did you see that!' It was certainly entertaining. The question is, was it real?

During a question-and-answer session at a seminar held by Grandmaster Ip Chun, a member of the audience posed the question:

'Is the dummy a tool for conditioning in order to help harden the limbs?' The answer was simple and was given in the form of a counter-question: 'If the dummy is just for conditioning, why does it have arms and legs?' Why spend a vast amount of money on a piece of equipment to destroy it?

Shaun's book brings us back to reality; it addresses the 'what', the 'when', the 'why' and the 'how'. This book, regardless of who is teaching, illustrates systematically the methods by which the Muk Yan Jong should be practised.

I greatly welcome Shaun's new book. It reminds us that Wing Chun is primarily a self-defence system, and the Muk Yan Jong is used as a tool to support it. In practising the Muk Yan Jong, it is necessary to gain accurate knowledge of the techniques before taking action. In his book, Sifu Shaun continually repeats the message that the Muk Yan Jong is a tool where one's mind is required to constantly translate thought into action.

Throughout the book, each teaching is supported by evidence as to why the Dummy must be played in a certain way to obtain the maximum and ultimate benefits. The book draws on the reader's logic and not on their emotion.

Sifu Garry McKenzie
The Wing Chun School, London, UK
www.thewingchunschool.com

When it comes to martial arts training aids, the Wooden Dummy is essential to the progress of every Wing Chun practitioner. It is like a training partner that never quits, and it is always ready for your next session and never allows you to become complacent. When used correctly, the Wooden Dummy will appear to come to life and guide you through the maze of understanding in order to assist your timing, speed, distance and power. It will do all this and a great deal more, but *only* if you use it correctly!

In order to get the most out of your Wooden Dummy training, you need to be educated by someone who knows how to use it and, more importantly, someone who knows what not to do. Shaun Rawcliffe, one of the Western world's most senior Wing Chun practitioners, is the ideal person. He has run the gauntlet, been taught by the best, spent his life in search of perfection and has an unequalled first-hand understanding of what is needed in order to get the most from every minute of your Wooden Dummy experience.

I have known Shaun for many years and can honestly say that he has dedicated his life to studying and understanding Wing Chun. There is nobody better suited to writing this book. I am sure you will gain a great deal from it and enjoy your experience of getting to know your Wooden Dummy. Happy training.

Paul S. Clifton
Publisher of *Combat*, *Fighters*,
Traditional Karate and *Taekwondo &*
Korean Martial Arts magazine

Acknowledgements

Many people, directly or indirectly, have influenced my Wing Chun over the years and I owe them all an acknowledgement of appreciation. These include Brian Hook, who provided me with a solid technical grounding in Wing Chun, and Stephen T. K. Chan, Simon Lau and Sam Kwok, all of who spent time honing and guiding my skills in the UK. In Hong Kong I have been fortunate to have met and discussed Wing Chun with numerous Wing Chun Sifus including Ip Ching, Wong Shun Leung, Chu Shong Tin, Siu Yuk Men, Lok Yiu, Leung Ting and many others.

I am equally grateful for the many hours spent discussing and practising Wing Chun with my Kung Fu brothers. They have assisted me greatly in the development of my Wing Chun, particularly Lo Tak On (Raymond), Leung Cheung Wai, Ho Po Kai, Leung Ting Kwok (Patrick) and Steve Cheung in Hong Kong, Yip Pui (Terence) in the USA, Ludo Delaloye in Switzerland and Colin Ward, Kwok Cheung, John Brogden and Karl Stanley in the UK. I thank you all and apologize to those whom I have not named; your time and assistance is much appreciated.

The one individual, however, who has had the greatest influence on my Wing Chun training and teaching, as well as on me as a person, is my Sifu and mentor, Ip Chun. He saw and drew out my potential, influenced my thinking and directed my approach to both training and teaching. His patience, humility, understanding and wisdom are an inspiration to myself and to all those who are fortunate enough to know and to train with him. He is truly a scholar and a gentleman. Ip Chun Sifu opened my eyes to Wing Chun training and teaching and gave my Wing Chun perspective, focus and meaning. In Sifu, I found a mentor, teacher and friend who was willing to spend his free time practising and discussing Wing Chun during my frequent trips to his Hong Kong home. No words can express my respect, admiration and thanks. I also thank his wife, Si-Mo for graciously accepting the many evenings that I trained in their living room until late at night and for providing me with many needed cups of Chinese tea.

I have had the privilege to meet many people through Wing Chun. I particularly thank Mr Paul Clifton, editor of *Combat* magazine, who has been a good friend for many years. He has advised me many times and has been my sounding board on more issues than I care to remember. I would also like to mention Garry McKenzie, the quiet man in Wing Chun, who focuses on his personal improvement and that of his students. He is a shining example of how a martial artist should conduct himself and is a reminder of the qualities that I hold dear and respect in true martial artists.

I thank all the students within the Midlands Wing Chun Kuen who have helped and supported me, taught me as much as I have taught them and driven me to train harder.

In particular, I thank the senior students and Instructors of the Midlands Wing Chun

Kuen: Steve Woodward, David Ackroyd-Jones, Steve Jones, Alberto Riccardi, Steve Shaw, Tariq Mahmood (Haji), Mohammed Akhtar, Harj Singh, Chris Bates, Ken Sayle, Umar Choudhury, Mark Poleon, Kieran McErlean and especially Kwok Wan for his translations and for the Chinese characters.

A special mention and thank you to Genea Rawcliffe and Mark Dunbar for writing their articles for inclusion in this book and for sharing their specialist subject knowledge.

Thanks also to Sifu David Ackroyd-Jones for the use of his studio for the Dummy photographs. As well as co-running the Cheltenham branch of the Midlands Wing Chun Kuen, David runs Physability, a rehabilitation centre specializing in spinal cord injury, head injury, multiple sclerosis and other paralysing conditions in Stroud, Gloucestershire (01453 755557).

I would like to thank my wife, Genea, who has endured for many years my evening and weekend classes and seminars. She has supported me on many training trips to Hong Kong and has recently spent many hours proofreading this document, correcting my grammar and advising me on its presentation and layout.

Finally, thanks to Steve Woodward (who co-runs the Cheltenham Wing Chun Kuen), Mark Poleon, Umar Choudhury and Genea Nicole Rawcliffe for their time, assistance and patience during the photo shoot in the UK (studio photos of the Wooden Dummy and studio partner photos by Lawrence Treanor, www.Lawrencetreanor.co.uk), and to Sifu John Brogden and Genea Nicole Rawcliffe (photography) for the photo shoot in Hong Kong.

This book is for and because of all of you.

Shaun Rawcliffe 2007
www.wingchun.co.uk

Fig 2   Steve, Shaun, Mark, Umar and Genea.

Preface

When I eventually wrote my first book, *Simply ... Wing Chun Kung Fu*, I had no idea how popular it would become. Writing a book purely about the Wing Chun system, rather than as a promotional tool for the author, struck a cord with many people in the Wing Chun world. Since then I have had many requests from my friends, training partners and peers to write a second book on the Wooden Dummy. This book is written in the same manner as my first book and shares the learning experience, insight and knowledge that I have been fortunate to gain through many years of training in Hong Kong with the eldest son of the late Grandmaster Ip Man.

A large part of the success of the first book was that it contained no photographs; each technique and position was illustrated with faceless line diagrams to show their triangulated structure and support. The diagrams provided a technical, illustrative and diagrammatical analysis of the core theories and principles of Wing Chun, without personal interpretation. In short the book wasn't about me or how I apply Wing Chun, it simply illustrated and defined the musculoskeletal structure that every Wing Chun student and instructor utilizes in the practice and deployment of their Wing Chun, regardless of their physique, gender or their interpretation of the applications of their techniques.

My major concern in writing a book on the Wooden Dummy was that it is not possible to illustrate the positions and movements of the Dummy with line diagrams, as the positions are more complex and need to be seen in a 'three-dimensional form', such as photographs.

Furthermore, in order to explain and demonstrate these movements fully, they need to be shown in some sort of practical application. This leads to the problem that one person's interpretation of an application of the movement may contradict another's interpretation. However, I have been unable to find a book on the Wooden Dummy that explains in depth the movements and the principles behind the movements, or gives examples of practical applications of the Dummy movements with concise explanations. In order to address these issues, I decided to write this book.

To progress and develop in Wing Chun, it is vital you understand what you are doing, how you should do it and the reason and theory behind each technique and position. I have tried to explain and demonstrate the techniques simply and clearly, using practical applications as *an* example of how they may be used, *not the* definitive way they should be applied. The sequence of the forms shown and discussed in this book reflects those taught to me in Hong Kong by my Sifu, Ip Chun, and taught by his father, Ip Man.

The sequence of the forms may not exactly match the sequences taught by other Sifus, but I hope that readers will appreciate and enjoy the content of this book, and not be distracted by the more trivial concern as to whether the names, spellings, translations of the techniques, or the sequence of the forms, match their own or those of their teacher.

I hope that readers will see past the 'that's not how we do it' mentality and appreciate the principles and theories behind the movements that are the common basis for all Wing Chun practitioners.

Great minds discuss ideas; average minds discuss events; small minds discuss people.
Eleanor Roosevelt

This book aims to provide a reference and checklist for every Wing Chun (Wing Tsun, Ving Tsun) practitioner. Consequently, each practitioner is then able to explore freely *their* applications, whilst still adhering to the basic core principles and shapes of the system. Remember that the structures in Wing Chun are simply tools, which, if fully understood in terms of shape, energy, structure and inherent lines of strength and weakness, can be deployed in a multitude of ways and scenarios.

In writing this second book, I have again chosen to spell 'Wing Chun' and the names of the techniques in the way of Ip Chun Sifu, translated for me by his senior students.

Throughout this book, I use the names of each technique or movement simply as a point of reference in order to discuss the shapes, structures and energies. The 'definitions' and their 'translations' are included simply to assist in gaining a greater understanding of the technique or movement.

It is not possible to learn the Dummy form from this, or any other, book; rather, I have written this book to supplement the knowledge gained through regular training with a qualified teacher. This book does not represent a conclusion in my training and teaching, which is continually improving and developing, nor does it make any pretence to be the definitive 'style' or methodology of the Wing Chun system; rather, it is the culmination of over twenty-eight years of research and training in the Wing Chun system.

This is a book for *all* Wing Chun students and instructors who are studying, practising or teaching the Wooden Dummy; it is not steeped in any martial arts mysticism; it does not discuss personal preferences; nor does it delve into the personalization that each student must undertake to make the system work for the individual. It is a detailed scientific and technical analysis of the Wing Chun Wooden Dummy form that I have learnt.

1   Introduction

What is Wing Chun Kung Fu?

Wing Chun is an event-driven, result-oriented self-defence system, originally developed in mainland China but refined in the sprawling concrete metropolis that is Hong Kong. Wing Chun is characterized by close-quarter simultaneous attack and defence hand techniques, utilization of only low kicks and simple, but efficient, footwork. It utilizes the natural triangulation of the human skeletal and muscular structure, in conjunction with efficient body mechanics, to give the techniques, positions and stances their inherent inner strength and hence their capability to withstand great force, eliminating the necessity to use and rely on size or strength. Wing Chun is suitable for anybody, regardless of age, gender, or physique.

The Wing Chun system contains three empty hand forms: Siu Nim Tao, Chum Kiu and Biu Tze. The hand techniques taught in the three forms are practised in Chi Sau (sticking hands), a unique exercise that is practised at close quarters (real fighting distance), to improve reflexes, responses, positions, angles, energies and hand techniques, achieving the best defence and counter-attack position. Chi Sau is a training exercise – a bridge between forms and fighting. It trains the reactions and direct responses to be natural, rather than fixed, so that you can explore freely and safely. Supplementing the forms and the Chi Sau are the 116 Wooden Dummy techniques (Muk Yan Jong), which include the eight basic kicking/leg techniques. Wing Chun training also incorporates two weapon forms – the six-and-a-half point long pole (Luk Dim Boon Kwun) and the eight chopping knives (Baat Cham Dao) – taught only when the student has a thorough knowledge and understanding of hand and footwork techniques.

The Wing Chun Code of Conduct

The late Grandmaster Ip Man set out the Wing Chun Code of Conduct to serve as a reminder to all Wing Chun practitioners that their art represents more than skill and fighting ability. It is preserved on an engraved plaque on the wall of the Ving Tsun Athletic Association in Hong Kong.

守 紀 律 崇 尚 武 德

Remain disciplined – uphold yourself ethically as a martial artist.

明 禮 義 愛 國 尊 親

Practise courtesy and righteousness – serve the community and honour your family.

愛 同 學 團 結 樂 群

Love your fellow students or classmates – be united and avoid conflicts.

節 色 慾 保 守 精 神

Limit your desires and pursuit of bodily pleasures – preserve the proper spirit.

勤 練 習 技 不 離 身

Train diligently and make it a habit – maintain your skills.

學 養 氣 救 濫 鬥 民

Learn to develop spiritual tranquillity – abstain from arguments and fights.

常 處 世 態 度 溫 民

Participate in society – be conservative, cultured and gentle in your manners.

扶 弱 小 以 武 輔 仁

Help the weak and the very young – use your martial skill for the good of humanity.

繼 光 緒 漢 持 祖 訓

Pass on the tradition – preserve this Chinese art and its Rules of Conduct.

Profile of the Author

Shaun began studying Wing Chun in 1979, following six years of Shotokan Karate. He studied Wing Chun in the UK under three Chinese Sifus for almost ten years before making the first of thirty trips to study in Hong Kong under Sifu Ip Chun in 1989.

Today, Shaun is one of the most senior representatives for Master Ip Chun: one of only eighteen people in the world to have earned an instructor's certificate from, and be allowed to officially represent, Sifu Ip Chun. He is a certified instructor within, and the certifying officer of, the Ip Chun Wing Chun Martial Arts Association.

Shaun is a permanent member of the Ip Chun Wing Chun Academy in Hong Kong, set up by students of Sifu Ip Chun, and a founding member of the European Ip Chun Wing Chun Association. He is registered with the Yip Man Martial Arts Association (Hong Kong), and is a member and certified registered instructor with the Ving Tsun Athletic Association in Hong Kong.

In the UK, Shaun is a certified coach with the British Council for Chinese Martial Arts and a member of the National Coaching Foundation (Sports Coach UK); the Sports Council recognizes both.

On 23 October 1999, Shaun was awarded a trophy as part of the Combat Hall of Fame Awards 'in recognition of his commitment and devotion to the development of martial arts in the United Kingdom and around the world'.

On 6 October 2001, he received a second Combat Hall of Fame Award 'in recognition of the contribution to gain martial arts practice greater popularity in both the UK and the world'.

Shaun's first book, entitled *Simply ... Wing Chun Kung Fu* and published by Crowood Press in September 2003, has received excellent critical reviews and is already into its second release in the UK. It has recently been translated into French and published in France.

Shaun has featured in many martial arts publications including *Combat*, *Fighters*,

Fig 3 Shaun and Ip Chun, Hong Kong, 2007.

Karate & Oriental Arts, *Samurai* (Italy) and *Qi* magazine, as well as non-martial arts publications such as *Later* magazine. He has also been a regular contributor on Wing Chun Kung Fu in *Combat* magazine. Shaun has featured in several books and publications including:

- *Simply … Wing Chun Kung Fu* by Sifu Shaun Rawcliffe
- *Grandmaster Yip Man Centenary Book* by the Ving Tsun Athletic Association (Hong Kong)
- *Wing Chun 50th Anniversary* by the Ving Tsun Athletic Association (Hong Kong)
- *Wing Chun Skill and Philosophy* by Grandmaster Ip Chun
- *Chinese WuShu Association Centenary* book by The Chinese WuShu Association.

Shaun has appeared in several videos/DVDs, assisting and demonstrating with his teacher, Ip Chun, including:

- *Ip Chun Wooden Dummy Techniques* by Legend Productions
- *Chinese Masters of Kung Fu* by Video Martial Arts International.

Shaun's Wing Chun demonstrations have featured on:

- *The 1st World Ving Tsun Conference 1999* VCD
- *World Superstars of the Martial Arts* by Video Martial Arts International
- *A World Martial Arts Extravaganza* by Stuart Promotions
  (He can be seen working as personal bodyguard for Miss Cynthia Rothrock in the latter two.)

In 2002, the Ip Man Tong Development Council, Foshan, China, made Shaun an 'Honorary Committee Member of Ip Man Tong'.

Training in Hong Kong in the Early 1990s

Everyone has his or her own, personal and unique experiences of Wing Chun training in Hong Kong. I was lucky because I went out to Hong Kong long before it was 'popular' or the thing to do. Today, training in Hong Kong is readily accessible and many schools, including my own, organize trips for their students to experience Wing Chun training amid the tower blocks, electronic shops and masses of people. Local students and overseas visitors attend the classes in equal numbers. However, during those first few years I rarely saw another Westerner training, and the odd one or two who did occasionally train were Hong Kong residents.

The first time I saw Sifu Ip Chun was in London in 1981 where he was the guest of honour of Sifu Simon Lau. However, I did not get to meet him or talk with him until June 1985, when he stayed with me for three days during which he gave a 3-hour seminar at my main school.

He had many qualities that made a lasting positive impression on me: a lack of ego, openness, a willingness to share his information, and he was the only Sifu I had ever met who was fully hands-on in his teaching. During his seminars, he practised Chi Sau with all the students regardless of their age, experience and physique. He could easily control and dominate them, not even needing to drive through and strike!

Between 1986 and 2000 Sifu returned a further twenty-six times to give seminars at my schools, often staying at my home for several days during his stay and giving me plenty of time and opportunity to practise and discuss Wing Chun with him. In August 2001, he came to the UK to be guest of honour at my wedding reception, and he was persuaded to give more seminars for my schools whilst staying with me.

My initial training in Hong Kong was the result of a conversation at my home following one of Sifu's seminars in February 1989, during which he recommended that I travel to Hong Kong to continue my studies with him. In May of that year, I boarded a Cathay Pacific flight to Hong Kong for a six-week intensive training trip that was to change my Wing Chun forever.

In 1989, training in Hong Kong was quite different from the way it is today. Beimo challenge matches were still occurring, though illegal. Beimo is a Hong Kong style of Kung Fu challenge between two different styles, usually on the rooftop, alley or secluded area of a park. Unlike the tournaments of today, these were real fights where rules and protective clothing were unknown. Because I was a Gwailo (literally 'ghost person' or 'white ghost' – Cantonese term for a white person) I was challenged on numerous occasions! Very few of the Wing Chun Sifus taught open classes, most only taught privately at their homes, on a rooftop or in one of the parks, and only the younger generation spoke fluent English, so translation and discussion was difficult.

At 64 years of age, Sifu had just semi-retired from his job and so was available to teach me during the day. Between 1989 and 1995, all my Wing Chun training in Hong Kong was at Sifu's home on the Ping Shek Estate in the Ngau Chi Wan area of New Kowloon, since he only taught privately in his home (his current daily classes did not start until around 1996). That meant up to an hour (depending on the traffic) travelling by bus or taxi from Repulse Bay on the south side of Hong Kong island (where I lived on that first trip) to Central, then by MTR (Hong Kong's underground) to the Choi Hung stop on Kowloon side. In subsequent years, I stayed in Wan Chai, which made the journey shorter.

In those days, the training emphasis was focused on efficient and practical applications. During the three-hour training sessions in the mornings, Sifu and I practised Chi Sau, the accent being on either Gung Lik (elbow energy) development or how to

Fig 4 Kowloon, Hong Kong, 1989.

use Chi Sau principles in a combat situation. Sifu taught and practised Chi Sau as an interactive fluid learning process, to refine and develop an awareness of the third and fourth stage of fighting: trapping hands and maintaining contact at the optimum fighting range. Chi Sau develops the sensitivity and contact reflexes in the arms, which allows the practitioner to assess the situation and to perceive and respond to an opponent's force and movements as soon as contact is gained. Chi Sau also develops close distance co-ordination, mobility, balance, timing, accuracy and the correct use of energy, which are essential in effective and efficient self-defence. Occasionally, Leung Ting Kwok, Law Kam Tak or Lam Seung Cheung partnered me so that Sifu could watch and monitor me. However, Sifu preferred the hands-on approach and spent most of the time practising with me whilst explaining to them what he was doing and why.

In the afternoon, I practised Siu Nim Tao, Chum Kiu or Biu Tze for the first hour, with Sifu observing and correcting. He taught the forms as a means of developing and refining the individual tools, positions and energies, whilst training stance development, simultaneous multiple awareness (eyes and ears) and developing a good powerful posture. Multiple awareness is the ability of the arms and legs to function independently of each other and independent of the body's natural biorhythmic rate, i.e. heart, pulse and breathing rate. The audio/visual senses are trained to listen and hear outside of the training room, and peripheral vision is developed by becoming aware of movement outside the normal visual range.

Siu Nim Tao training focused primarily on the stance, posture, elbow energy and triangulated structure in conjunction with developing a basic set of primary and secondary tools. Chum Kiu focused primarily on stance work, footwork, upper and lower body co-ordination, passive centreline recovery, and receiving and intercepting techniques. Finally, Biu Tze focused on energy usage, recovery techniques (Gow Gup Sau) and active and aggressive recovery of the centreline.

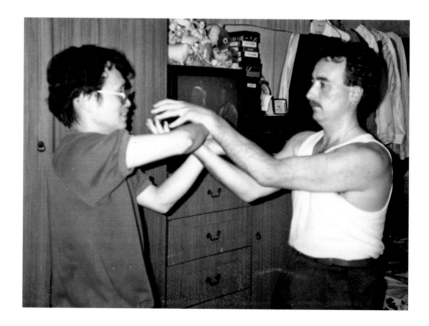

Fig 5   Chi Sau practice at Sifu's home, 1989.

For a further hour in the afternoon, I practised and explored the practical applications of the 'tools' from the forms. Sifu demonstrated their use on me, and then I practised on the students Sifu Ip Chun brought to partner me. The purpose of these drills and exercises was to improve or enhance the practical applications and to assist in remembering what movement, or combination of movements, the associated sensations and the musculoskeletal structures required to perform those movements, all of which must be transferred into the motor areas of the brain and stored in the long-term memory. This process is known as consolidation; it requires attention, repetition and associative ideas.

The final hour of the afternoon session was dedicated to fighting applications, which were taught in the form of one attack/one defend. This teaches how to actually use and apply the techniques that have been refined within the forms and interactively refined within the drills. Fighting applications refine the first and second stages of self-defence. The first stage, through much practice, is to recognize the form and direction of the attack, and the second is to bridge the gap and make contact, simultaneously defending and striking.

Sifu's flat is modest, so whilst Sifu and I practised Chi Sau, forms or fighting applications in the centre of the room, his eldest son would lie on Sifu's bed trying to watch TV. Sifu's wife, Si-Mo, would sit in the doorway watching us and providing many welcome cups of Bo Lei Cha (Chinese Tea). Despite the fact that the temperature was often 30 degrees or more and the relative humidity over 90 per cent, the air conditioning was rarely on, although the ceiling fan did move the warm humid air – downwards!

Every evening I studied the Wooden Dummy (Muk Yan Jong) and the Knives (Baat Cham Dao) for a further three hours.

Sifu's Wooden Dummy, which originally belonged to Ip Man, is located in what is, in effect, a large enclosed balcony, opposite the kitchen area. There was no air conditioning or ceiling fan in this area, so it was hot and humid; the window was often open, so the hot draught was mixed with the sound of the traffic thirteen floors below and the sound of aircraft (Sifu's flat overlooked the cargo terminal of the old Kai Tak airport).

I studied the Wooden Dummy in sections at first, drilling each of the sections in turn, checking my positions and movements. Sifu gave a running commentary in Cantonese, constantly physically corrected me, and then demonstrated himself. On the occasions when there was an English-speaking translator, I bombarded Sifu with questions only to be overwhelmed by the flow of answers. Once I had learned all eight sections of the Dummy, I drilled and drilled the individual core movements for hours at a time, Sifu sitting in his canvas director's chair watching and advising, whilst smoking his pipe. The next step was to practise the Dummy movements repeatedly without the Dummy, to improve fluidity. Finally, Sifu encouraged me to practise freely on the Dummy without reference to the sequence of the form, flowing from one position to the next logical position. On some evenings, one of Sifu's students, Leung Ting Kwok, joined us to translate and Sifu and I discussed various aspects of the Dummy: energy, footwork, position, kicks and so on.

It was on one of these evenings that I was first shown the original and unedited version of the 8mm movie of Grandmaster Ip Man demonstrating Siu Nim Tao, Chum Kiu and finally Muk Yan Jong (Wooden Dummy) filmed at his home in Tung Choi Street, Mong Kok, shortly before his death in 1972. The original film shows how easily tired Grandmaster Ip Man became whilst performing the Dummy, due to ill health.

Fig 6 Hong Kong training, 1989.

Whilst watching the film, Sifu Ip Chun, who was there throughout the filming, gave me a running commentary, pointing out various aspects of the Dummy practice, laughing at the fact that some people thought these were 'secret' techniques, where in fact the actions were simply due to Grandmaster Ip Man's fragility at that time.

Some evenings I practised the Baat Cham Dao (Knives). I first learnt the moves section by section, later drilling the movements repeatedly until my wrists, forearms and shoulders burnt with fatigue. Sifu and I spent hours discussing the Knives, the benefits of training and the practicality, if any, of the weapons in a modern society. On some occasions, when it was unbearably hot in Sifu's home, we practised outside in a basketball court adjacent to the flats. On one of these occasions, I noticed several elderly men watching intently from a bench nearby. Sifu told me that these men lived in the same apartment block as him and were fellow students of Grandmaster Ip Man. He added

that though they did not teach Wing Chun, they were fascinated to watch a Gwailo practising advanced Wing Chun techniques.

I learnt much about Sifu as a person whilst chatting over 'Yum Cha'. As well as being an accomplished martial artist of the highest degree, he is also a man of extraordinary wisdom and energy. His interests extend far beyond Wing Chun, incorporating literature, poetry, music and, of course – football! Despite our language barrier, we have had endless discussions, not only about Wing Chun, but on a vast variety of subjects, ranging from Chinese culture to British politics. I think that our inability to speak each other's language well has been beneficial, because I have had to learn to interpret Sifu's actions rather than just listen to his words.

The mediocre teacher tells. The good teacher explains. The superior teacher demonstrates. The great teacher inspires.

William Ward

I visited Hong Kong twice a year, every year between 1989 and 1996 to train at Sifu's home. Each time training took a similar format, although sometimes there was no training on a Thursday, as Sifu went walking from Shatin to Sai Kung (no mean feat). My fourth trip, in the summer of 1990, was sometimes disrupted, as Sifu would stay up till the early hours of the morning to watch England play live in the World Cup!

Since my initial visit to Hong Kong, I have made over thirty trips to study with Sifu. On several of these trips, I have taken groups of my own students with me to share the experience. This has allowed me to sit back and watch Sifu teaching, and I am still amazed at how simple he makes everything look.

I recorded every training session at Sifu's home, and over the years have built up an extensive catalogue of videotapes. After every training session, the journey back to my accommodation (an hour on my first trip and at least half an hour on subsequent trips) gave me ample time to reflect on that day's training and make copious notes. Those notes and videos culminated in my first and this second book.

The palest ink is better than the best memory.

Chinese proverb

Fig 7   Hong Kong training group, 2007.

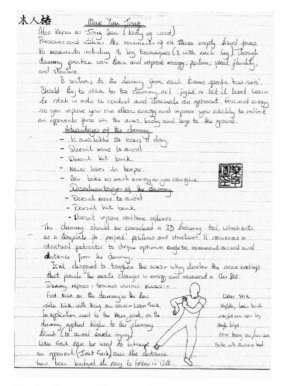

Fig 8   Scanned image of training notes from Hong Kong training, 1989.

What are Forms?

Forms (Kuen Tou), some call them patterns or katas, are a solo performance of a preset sequence of movements, which practise, refine and instil a set of structures, energies, body mechanics, principles and techniques. There are no direct applications of these movements, and the forms do not teach the student how to apply those techniques as they cannot, nor are they intended to, represent the fluid, unpredictable interaction with another person whilst under the threat, duress and stress that is self-defence.

The sequence and order of the movements within the Wing Chun forms is somewhat irrelevant, in the same way that the order of the letters in the English alphabet is immaterial. In the English alphabet no three or more consecutive letters form any word; similarly no string of movements within the Wing Chun forms define a specific fighting sequence. Instead of looking to the forms to teach combinations or to provide answers to problems in application, the forms should be regarded as a physical alphabet, a collection of tools logically collated so that the movements flow smoothly and logically from one position to the next.

The solo practice of the Wing Chun forms provides the practitioner with a preset list of positions and movements that enables him or her to train for 'perfect' positions, something that is not possible when relating the techniques to a partner or opponent. As soon as the practitioner trains with a partner, his 'perfect' positions will be compromised because he will have to compensate for his partner's size, reach, power, momentum and so on. In a real confrontation, a practitioner's positions and techniques are corrupted even further, as he has to compensate further for other factors such as an opponent's aggression, the possibility of multiple attackers, unfamiliar territory and whether the attackers are armed or unarmed.

Once learned within the forms, each of the techniques, structures and movements must be analysed and then practised with a partner in order to appreciate the musculoskeletal framework that gives them their inherent strength, the correct body mechanics that make them fast and efficient, and to develop an understanding of the strengths and weaknesses of each technique and structure.

2 The Wing Chun Wooden Dummy

Muk – Cantonese term meaning **wood** *n.*, the trunks of trees that have been cut and prepared.
Yan – Cantonese term meaning **man** *n.*, a human being, considered representative of mankind.
Jong – Cantonese term meaning **stake** *n.*, a stick or metal bar driven into the ground.

Introduction

Muk Yan Jong literally translates 'wood man stake', but is usually referred to as the Wooden Dummy or the Jong. As a training aid, the Wooden Dummy is not unique to Wing Chun; Choy Li Fut, for example, also has a Wooden Dummy form. However, the Wing Chun Wooden Dummy and the movements of the form are unique and were specifically designed to practise and develop Wing Chun skills.

In order to benefit from the Dummy training, a student must first have a thorough understanding of Siu Nim Tao, Chum Kiu and Biu Tze (Saam Kuen Tou) because the basic techniques practised and refined on the Dummy are first learnt and developed in the empty hands forms.

> The moves of the Wooden Dummy are all good for fighting. However, those moves are actually formed by the basic moves of Siu Nim Tao, Chum Kiu and Biu Tze. They are not uniquely owned by the Wooden Dummy.
>
> *Chu Shong Tin*

Whilst some instructors place too much emphasis on teaching and training the Dummy, others place too little. The Wooden Dummy training is an important part of the Wing Chun system and, as such, it has great benefits; equally, it has some drawbacks. One major benefit is that it is available twenty-four hours a day and, unlike training partners, it never sleeps, gets tired, hits back or tries to argue with you. The disadvantages are that it does not move like an opponent or partner, it does not react, it is not unpredictable like a live opponent and, of course, it does not hit back!

With constant practice on the Dummy, it is possible to develop excellent positioning, structure and energy, whilst moving fluidly and swiftly, maintaining a powerful stance, supporting a good body posture and efficient body mechanics.

> The main purpose of the Dummy is to improve structure.
>
> *Ip Chun*

History of the Wing Chun Wooden Dummy

The Wing Chun Wooden Dummy allegedly originated from the Siu Lam (Shaolin) monastery of Mt Sung in the Honan province of China, where it is said that there was a hall or corridor of Dummies (some say 108 Dummies) through which the Shaolin

Fig 9   Grandmaster Ip Man practising on the Dummy, 1972.

Fig 10   A young Shaun practising on the Dummy, 1984.

Monks must pass. These Dummies had moveable arms and legs, controlled by the monks, which were used to test the skills of the departing monks as they left the temple. This became known as 'Wooden Dummy alley'.

Whether this is true or not is not known, but we do know that the original Dummy was a long stake partly buried in the ground (Dei Jong). Sometimes referred to as a 'dead' or fixed Dummy, this type of Dummy hardly moves and it is still in use in Fatshan in the Guangdong province of China.

When the late Wing Chun Grandmaster Ip Man moved to Hong Kong in 1949 and started to teach Wing Chun there, it was impractical in the modern high-rise apartment blocks to use a stake in the ground, so the Dummy was fixed on to a timber frame, stood on the floor and fixed to a solid wall.

Known as the 'live' Dummy, this provides some degree of movement when force is applied to it due to flexing in the horizontal struts on which it is supported. This flexing reduces the risk of impact injury (although the Dummy is not for hitting) through forceful contact and returns some of that force back into the practitioner, testing their stance and arm structure.

Today there are many varieties of Dummies – wooden, plastic, and even metal. Some are supported on wooden frames, some on springs, some are freestanding and some even fit into a doorframe.

Traditionalists insist that a live Wooden Dummy is still the best, yet if you cannot install one inside your home, then perhaps a plastic one, which is impervious to the elements, or a wooden freestanding one may prove a better buy. Although each Dummy is unique and must be height-adjusted to suit the individual, the proportions, sizes and positions of the arms and leg should be constructed to standard specifications, which are suited to the movements and positions of the Wing Chun system and to the human anatomy. As long as the Dummy is constructed and proportioned correctly, the choice of Dummy depends on your circumstances, your personal preferences and the cost.

Wooden Dummy Design

Ideally, the live Dummy should be suspended about 6in (152mm) above the floor, although the actual height of the Dummy from the floor depends on the height of the practitioner. The trunk should be between 7½in and 9in (200–228mm) in diameter and approximately 4½ft to 5ft (1365–1524mm) in height. As you face the Dummy in stance, the upper left arm of the Dummy should be at your shoulder height and the lower central arm at navel height; the 'knee' on the Dummy's leg should ideally be at the same height as the practitioner's knee when standing with one leg forward.

The specific dimensions and proportions of the Dummy represent an attacker, a three-dimensional training tool, but in order to benefit from training on the Dummy it has to be used intelligently and with a good understanding of the structures and the principles of Wooden Dummy training. For example, when facing the Dummy the two upper arms appear to be splaying outwards, yet they are said to represent an attacker's punches. In reality, as you face and look at the Dummy, the left-hand-side arm usually represents an opponent throwing a left cross. Similarly, the right-hand-side arm represents a right-hand cross. However, in

Fig 11   Dummy from the front.

Fig 12   Dummy from the side.

opponent's force and momentum and to obtain an advantageous position. Footwork is improved through practice on the Dummy by stepping in, out and around the body and the leg of the Dummy. This footwork utilizes all the basic footwork drills and stances of the Wing Chun system developed in the three empty hand forms. Furthermore, the footwork positions must be correct and the legs powerful in order to be able to apply powerful and accurate kicks on to the Dummy. The stance must be solid and powerful when force (not a strike) is applied to the Dummy, either when kicking or using the hands. An almost equal force is returned as the Dummy hardly moves on its frame. If the stance is weak or badly positioned, this will show.

Newton ([1687] 1999), in his 'Third Law of Motion', states:

> Whenever a body exerts a force on another body, the latter exerts a force of equal magnitude and opposite direction on the former.

Which is more commonly expressed as:

> To every action there is an equal and opposite reaction.

Speed and Fluidity

Speed on the Wooden Dummy is developed through familiarity of the techniques and the practice of flowing smoothly between the techniques. At first, the Dummy should be practised slowly, to check and refine each position and structure. However, once these are being performed correctly, the movements and the flow between the structures can be done more quickly as long as the positions and structures are not compromised. Flowing smoothly and quickly between positions means that there are less gaps or pauses between the techniques for an attacker to exploit.

Maintaining Contact

One of the main aspects of Dummy training is to stick to the Dummy and maintain contact as much as possible. When it is not possible to remain in contact, the practitioner should regain contact as quickly as possible taking the shortest route, but not by crashing on to the Dummy's arms with excessive force.

> The moment you pull your arm back, you leave an opening to be attacked.
>
> *Ip Ching*

Maintaining contact with the Dummy as much as possible enables the practitioner to apply forwards elbow energy into the body of the Dummy via the arms as well as directly as a strike.

> Do not chase your opponent's hands; always attack their centreline.
>
> *Wing Chun Maxim*

On a more practical level, hitting the arms (or the body) of the Wooden Dummy hard is neither beneficial nor healthy. Wing Chun uses enhanced sensitivity to 'feel' minute changes in the position, tension and energy of an opponent through contact. Hard impact, however, causes contusions, and possibly a haematoma, dulls the sensitivity and, in the long term, may damage or kill the nerve receptors. A recent new study in America on professional baseball catchers' hands found that, despite recent improvements in glove design, repetitive pounding is causing long-term, irreversible damage to many catchers' hands, especially their index fingers.

> We think that the repetitive impact over time causes scarring around the digital nerves and arteries, and some of the microvessels.
>
> *Dr Andrew Koman*
> *Professor of Orthopaedic Surgery at Wake*
> *Forest University School of Medicine*

29

According to Ip Chun, his father Ip Man told him:

> The trainee who makes the noisiest movements while having a drill with the Dummy does not make the best use of it, though his movement might look splendid to a layman. A good trainee aims at clinging his arms to the Dummy, with each of his movements shaking the Dummy. [This is the] correct way of using it. He should bear in mind that the Dummy is not designed to strengthen his bridge-arms, but to train him to take up the most suitable position, to use the most useful techniques and to adopt the best tactic for dealing with variations of movements while fighting with a real opponent. Therefore, what is most important is to learn to take up the correct position as required at each movement and to learn to keep on clinging his arms to the Dummy – that is to say to have his arms touching the Dummy or to keep them as close to them as possible in every moment, in the same way as he would do to keep the opponent's arms within the touch of his own arms in a real fight, so as to minimize the opponent's range of movements.

Muscle Resistance Training on the Dummy

Elbow energy (Gung Lik) can be developed and refined on the Wooden Dummy by resistance training, which involves muscle contraction through pushing, pressing or pulling against an immovable object or a resistance. This increases muscle strength and speed by forcing the muscles to push against, or hold, a position for a certain length of time. The pressure against the resistance provides stimulation for muscle tissues, increases nervous conductivity and the ability to contract more muscle fibre.

When training on the Wooden Dummy, muscle resistance training and development is achieved by maintaining a forward

Fig 16   Grandmaster Ip Man practising on the Dummy, 1972.

energy from the elbow along the Dummy's arms towards the centre of the Dummy. The Dummy moves away as the forward pressure is applied. However, the resistance increases as the frame reaches its limit of flexibility, providing an isotonic resistance. When the Dummy cannot move any further away the resistance remains constant, providing an isometric resistance.

Through isometric and isotonic exercise, the body begins to recruit and activate more and more motor units to help maintain this contraction. There are two different types of muscle fibres – slow twitch (Type I) muscle and fast twitch (Type II) muscle fibre. Fast twitch muscle fibres can be subdivided into Type IIa and Type IIb. The fast twitch muscle fibres are responsible for giving the martial artist his speed, accelerative force and power. Fast twitch fibres are thought to be 10 times faster than slow fibres.

Isometric Definition

The term 'isometric' comes from the Greek 'iso', meaning equal or same, and 'metric', meaning measure or distance – maintaining the same measure, dimension or length. Resistance to isometric contractions involves maximal contractions of the muscle against the Dummy, but can also involve holding a joint position against a sub-maximal contraction. Hislop and Perrine (1967) described isometric exercise as muscular contractions against a load that is fixed or immovable or is simply too much to overcome.

Isotonic Definition

The term 'isotonic' comes from the Greek 'iso', meaning equal or same, and 'tonos', meaning tone – maintaining equal (muscle) tone. It refers to a muscle contraction, either eccentric or concentric, which is not speed limited, and where the tension remains constant as the muscle contracts and shortens, giving movement. However, although 'isotonic' is the term used most frequently to describe fixed-resistance variable-speed exercise, 'isoinertial' is a more accurate description of this type of movement (Abernethy *et al.* 1995).

Note. When specifically training and developing elbow energy (Gung Lik), it is recommended that you maintain the forward pressure for 8 to 10 seconds. It is equally important, however, to maintain a strong, correctly structured stance and a good vertical posture as developed in the practice of Siu Nim Tao and Chum Kiu (*see* article below).

In order to provide a more insightful and accurate reflection of muscle resistance training on the Dummy, I have included an article written by one of my students, Dr Mark Dunbar.

'Wooden Dummy Training From a Medical Viewpoint' by Dr Mark Dunbar

As a UK-based orthopaedic surgeon, I have some experience of thinking about the body from an anatomical and biomechanical point of view. However, any attempt to discuss or explain a Chinese martial art that was developed using Chinese philosophy and terminology is fraught with difficulty.

Moreover, the intricate scientific understanding of how the body works has been investigated more from the point of view of treating disease rather than from understanding normal and athletic function.

For example, we know quite a lot about how to treat severe arthritis of the knee and much research and design has gone into producing the artificial total knee replacements that have been used for the last few decades. However, it is only in the last few years that we have gained a more detailed insight into how the normal knee joint actually moves. This same lack of understanding extends into most other areas of normal function, which means that my attempts to explain the processes at work in Wing Chun are a mixture of fact, theory and supposition. However, there are likely to be some interesting things happening to our bodies as we embark on the journey to develop our Wing Chun skill.

Current explanations of how the brain and body interact require in-depth knowledge of a variety of medically related fields, including anatomy, biomechanics, neuroscience, physiology and psychology. However, without focusing at that level of detail here, it seems clear that the overall aim of this interaction is to allow us to function in the best way possible for any given task. The Wooden Dummy is a constant and reliable training 'partner' in that it does not change its physical properties over time and remains relatively motionless. Human training partners vary their responses, which is useful for certain aspects of training, but the Wooden Dummy is extraordinarily useful because it is the only tool that allows us to practise and measure ourselves against a constant.

The single technique that I have chosen to elucidate some of the underlying processes is that of Tan Da as utilized and deployed in the first and second sections of the Dummy form. Tan Sau is applied to one of the Dummy's arms whilst force is applied simultaneously to the Dummy's body with the other open hand (Wan Jeung).

Let us briefly recap the possible actions of the muscles involved. Muscles carry out work when they attempt to contract. Understanding the different types of contractions is crucial to understanding how the use of the Wooden Dummy impacts on our Wing Chun ability.

- **concentric contraction** – the muscle actually shortens as it contracts
- **eccentric contraction** – the muscle attempts to contract to resist lengthening
- **isometric contraction** – the muscle contracts, but remains the same length.

You may read about *isotonic* and *isokinetic* contractions, but they are not required for the specific descriptions here. An isotonic contraction is one where the muscle contracts under a constant load, and an isokinetic contraction is the label attached to a contraction that occurs at a constant speed.

Two other important terms are *agonist*, which refers to the prime moving muscle group and *antagonist*, referring to the opposing muscle group.

What happens when we train our basic punches in basic stance without using a wall bag? Let us try to simplify it as much as possible and ignore what is happening across the shoulder joint and below the shoulder girdle. During the first part of the movement, as you extend at the elbow, you are staying relaxed and punching with speed until you reach your natural endpoint. During this part of the movement, your triceps muscle group (agonist) are contracting *concentrically* and your biceps muscle group (antagonist) should be relaxed. Eventually, as you reach your natural endpoint where your elbow becomes straight, there must be a deceleration, which is caused by both static and dynamic elements. The static elements are structures such as the fibrous elbow joint capsule and the bony olecranon. These are unlikely to be modified by training. The dynamic elements include all of the elbow flexors – biceps

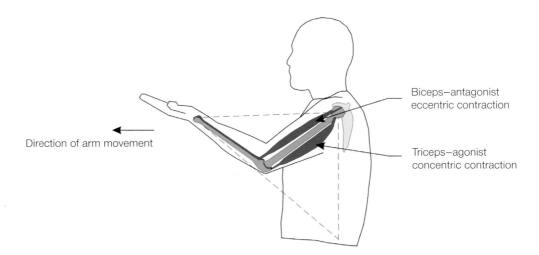

Direction of arm movement

Biceps–antagonist
eccentric contraction

Triceps–agonist
concentric contraction

Fig 17   Diagram showing agonist and antagonist muscle usage.

brachii, brachialis – and interestingly a few of the forearm muscles that cross the elbow joint. At the end of the punch, these undergo an *eccentric* contraction.

The functioning of these dynamic elements can be changed significantly with training. There has been no published work on the muscle dynamics of the Wing Chun punch, but I suspect that the majority of the work done at the endpoint of the punch is actually done by these forearm muscles in conjunction with the static elements because we aim to keep the biceps as relaxed as possible. This has the additional benefit of helping to stabilize the wrist. However, because at this endpoint we employ these elbow extension antagonists, this punch does not have the same characteristics as a punch used in a real-life situation. In a real-life situation, your opponent defines the endpoint for you. Apart from stabilizing the forces going across the wrist and elbow joints, there is no need to try and counteract your own punching force. It is much better to transfer all of that force into your opponent.

Now that we have explored what is likely to be happening with the basic punch, we can reflect on the differences that arise when we think about how we interact with the Wooden Dummy. The most important difference is that when we make contact with the Dummy (with Tan Sau rather than the basic punch) it provides a natural resistance at the endpoint. There is no need for the antagonists to be active and therefore this movement replicates much more closely, what should be happening in a real-life situation against a human opponent. With no antagonists working against the elbow extensors, a maximal and more efficient force can be more easily achieved.

We now refer back to our technique – the Tan Da from the first and second sections. What is going on with respect to the Wan Jeung? This is analogous to the basic punch, but it gets more interesting when we

consider what else is happening in the rest of the body. When the palm is in contact with the Dummy's body and energy is applied, the Dummy moves only slightly and all of the reactant force has to be absorbed by the practitioner. This means that the shoulder girdle, spine, pelvic girdle and lower limbs have to remain fixed and unmoved in order to allow transmission of force into the Dummy. This is achieved by mainly *isometric* (*see* earlier) contractions of all of the muscles around these joints. Isometric contractions allow a stable platform from which to deliver any technique. Without the stable platform our body structure may collapse and the maximum, most efficient delivery of force will not be possible. Training on the Dummy improves one's ability to perform these contractions and improves the ability to deliver techniques from a stable platform.

When we train in any activity, our bodies adapt so that the muscle fibres that we commonly use become more efficient at making our chosen movements. The nerve impulses that cause the muscles to contract become more efficient and the necessary coordinated instructions to move multiple muscle groups becomes hard-wired into the supplementary motor cortex (otherwise known as 'muscle memory'). Although working on the Dummy can develop energy, training is more about learning how to transfer energy efficiently. There are many other training activities that help increase muscle power, but none do so in such a technique-specific manner.

Yet again, even considering all of the descriptions presented before, there is another level of complexity because most Dummies are not completely static. Different makes of Dummy vary, but they all have some element of 'give'. Some of the traditional ones move considerably and exert a force back on the practitioner that is proportionate to the distance that it has been moved. This means that each movement then becomes a complex interplay between dynamic concentric contractions of the extremities and isometric contractions of the central and stabilizing muscle groups. The practitioner sets the level of intensity by choosing to use a certain amount of force, and that force, when it is reflected back, must be equally absorbed by these stabilizing muscles.

The magnitude and duration of application of force to the dummy has been a contentious issue, with some proponents demonstrating techniques by hitting the dummy hard. I feel that this somewhat misses the point because the previously described main benefits of training the whole body structure to transmit force efficiently and quickly can be gained just as easily by applying short, sharp force into the dummy from contact. The controlled application of force allows the practitioner not only to explore and improve on their ability over time, but also to recognize and learn the limitations of force that their body structure can withstand. This is very important. If uncontrolled maximal forces are used, learning is less likely to occur. Wing Chun develops the ability to be sensitive to the magnitude and direction of force and to redirect appropriately. Using our example of Tan Sau, the practitioner will learn, over time, how much force he can apply into the Dummy's arm whilst still maintaining structure in his arm or stance. The subconscious recognition of this limit allows him to make adjustments quickly in real-life scenarios. As training occurs and the practitioner's ability increases, more force can be applied without detriment.

The most useful elements of training do not have anything to do with body conditioning or bone strengthening. More frequent and useful training can occur if the bones of the fist and forearm are not constantly trying to heal from their last assault. From a medical perspective the risks of developing stress fractures and repetitive strain injuries with this type of training is high. Stress fractures arise from persistent aggravation of the microfractures that occur in any bone that has been pushed beyond its limits. Normal bone will adapt over time and remodel itself so that it becomes more efficient at withstanding common stresses. However, if not given adequate time to heal, there may be unnecessarily long recovery periods where training cannot progress.

Returning once again to the Tan Sau technique, we can see that apart from the use of correct body structure as required by the particular angles and shapes on the Dummy, the use of the Dummy teaches us to apply force in an efficient way. At the same time, it improves and fine-tunes the other elements of body movement and structure to allow the whole body to become efficient at delivering the technique.

The Dummy is a complex and intriguing training tool. Here we have only touched upon one technique, frozen it in time and looked at it from an almost static standpoint. A detailed explanation of all 116 techniques is currently not feasible. A full and completely scientific explanation of even one technique would involve the use of a three-dimension motion lab and electromyographic recording equipment. None of this work has yet been done. However, the suppositions that I have made here are one explanation of some of the underlying processes and move some way towards a Western explanation of Chinese concepts. Whilst there is still some doubt over the exact processes, the fact remains that training on the Dummy works and significantly improves one's ability. Unravelling the reasons why is of secondary importance to putting in the training time.

Dr Mark Dunbar MA, BM, BCh, MRCS trains at the Hall Green branch of the Midlands Wing Chun Kuen under the supervision of Sifu Rawcliffe. He is a UK-trained orthopaedic surgeon, currently practising in the West Midlands.

3   The Wooden Dummy Form

In the Dummy form taught by Wing Chun's Grandmaster Ip Man, and practised by the majority of Wing Chun practitioners, there are 116 movements in the form. Originally, there were 140 movements, but the Grandmaster consolidated them first to 108, and then later he increased the number of techniques to 116 to include 16 training techniques for kicks and leg usage.

The Dummy form, however, is most often referred to as the 108 Wooden Dummy movements because the number 108 is considered lucky in Chinese culture, having significance in Chinese lunar mathematics, superstition and religion. The number 108 also has special significance in Buddhism. It is no coincidence, therefore, that Wing Chun's empty hand forms – Siu Nim Tao, Chum Kiu and Biu Tze – each have 108 movements.

The Wooden Dummy Maxims

- There are 108 movements for the Wooden Man; repeated practice brings proper use of energy.
- Steps vary and always maintain close contact with the Wooden Man.
- Power starts from the heart and shoots towards the centreline of the Muk Yan Jong.
- Up, down, back and forth, the movements are continuous.
- Power improvement cannot be predicted.
- The arm bridge sticks to the hands of the Wooden Man while moving;

sticking power, when achieved, will be a threatening force.
- Energy can be released in the intended manner; use of the line and position will be correct and hard to defeat.

The 108 (116) movements of the Dummy are subdivided into eight sections; the first four sections based around the movements of Siu Nim Tao and Chum Kiu and the last four sections around Biu Tze movements. Within each section, the techniques learned and practised are categorized into three distinct levels:

1. **Primary techniques**
    The primary techniques are the core technique or techniques particular to that section.
2. **Secondary techniques**
    The secondary techniques complement or relate to the primary techniques and should still be considered core techniques.
3. **Tertiary techniques**
    Finally, the tertiary techniques are those techniques that accompany the primary and secondary to make up the sequence of each section. They do not have the priority of the core techniques; however, these are still important techniques and must be practised carefully and correctly.

There are several key points to make before describing the Wooden Dummy form.

- The specific sequence explained and illustrated in this book is the Dummy form as taught by Grandmaster Ip Man to his eldest son, Ip Chun. Subsequently Sifu Ip Chun both taught and explained it to me in great detail between 1989 and 1995, during which time I kept a meticulous record, by way of video recordings and notes, to which I have referred frequently. This meticulous approach has ensured the accuracy of the content of this book and the explanations within.
- When teaching the Dummy form, it is common to 'punctuate' or separate the individual sections using a double Jut Sau movement, followed by a double Tok Sau movement. These movements serve no other purpose and are not counted within the 116 movements, so I have chosen not to include them within this book.
- All angles referred to are approximations and are relative to the Wooden Dummy frame assuming it is a 'live' Dummy, or relative to a line perpendicular to the Dummy's leg/lower arm, assuming it is a freestanding Dummy.
- When describing the hand techniques on the Dummy, the area between the upper Dummy's arms is referred to as the 'inside gate' of the Dummy; the area outside the Dummy's arms is referred to as the 'outside gate'.
- All descriptions referring to the left arm or right arm of the Dummy are from the Wing Chun practitioner's point of view – facing the Dummy.
- The photographs used to explain and demonstrate the Wooden Dummy applications are shown as *an* example of how they may be used, *not the* definitive way they should be applied. There are many different ways in which each of the techniques can be used in a variety of applications and variations; it is not possible to discuss, detail or illustrate all of them.

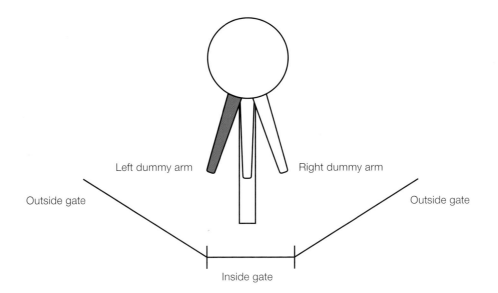

Left dummy arm   Right dummy arm

Outside gate   Outside gate

Inside gate

Fig 18   Dummy definitions.

Muk Yan Jong Fa

Key Stages in the Learning Process
In keeping with the significance of the number three, considered lucky in Chinese culture, there are three key stages when learning and practising the Dummy form:

1. *Muk Yan Jong Fa* – practise each section movement by movement, until fluent and proficient in the use and application of each of the movements, and the position required while making each movement and whilst changing from one movement to another.
2. *Mor Jong* – the action of constant and repetitive polishing. This stage requires the practitioner to repeat and repeat the core techniques of each section to refine and develop the skills to apply each technique correctly and powerfully without conscious thought.
3. *Goo Ding Ying Sic, Doh Mo Goo Ding Ying Sic* – the final stage (literally fixed form to no fixed form) is to free the practitioner of the restraints of the form and to apply the techniques within each section in any logical sequence.

The prerequisites of Wooden Dummy training are patience, conscientiousness and determination. Through correct practice and understanding, the Dummy enables the Wing Chun practitioner to develop a deep and thorough comprehension of the correct body position and structure required to apply techniques powerfully and successfully.

Beginning the Form
Before actually starting the movements of the form, it is essential to open the correct stance. This is an adaptation of 'Yee' Gee Kim Yeung Ma taught in Siu Nim Tao. It is an adaptation, or rather an application, because although it is opened in the same manner as that in Siu Nim Tao to ensure the stance width is correct for the individual practitioner, the feet should be parallel, rather than rotated inwards. The optimum distance from the Dummy is where the practitioner can reach the Dummy with the palms and slightly bent arms whilst maintaining a vertical posture and the correct stance. This distance must be checked and, if necessary, adjusted before starting the form. If the starting distance is incorrect, this will adversely affect the structure, posture and position of the movements and techniques within the form (*see* Fig 19).

Prior to beginning the sequence of the Dummy form, an 'on-guard' or By Jong position may be adopted, usually with a left arm lead (*see* Fig 20).

Section 1

This section introduces three techniques unique to the Dummy form (they are not in Siu Nim Tao, Chum Kiu or Biu Tze): Man Geng Sau, Kwun Sau and Kau Sau.

Man Geng Sau
Man – Cantonese term meaning **neck.**
Geng – Cantonese term meaning **pull.**
Sau – Cantonese term meaning **hand** or **arm**.

Man Geng Sau uses the Jut Sau elbow energy, as trained in the Siu Nim Tao form, to deploy a sharp and powerful impact force on to the cervical vertebrae (C1–C7), causing acute cervical sprains (whiplash) or trauma due to the resulting hyperextension as the neck moves back beyond normal limits.

To maximize the power and effect of Man Geng Sau and to give as much protective cover as possible to the Wing Chun practitioner, the elbow should be drawn in close to the centreline so that the shape of the arm resembles Fook Sau, again as trained in Siu Nim Tao. The effects of the sharp impact to

Fig 19   Check the correct distance before starting the form.

Fig 20   By Jong or ready position.

the back of the neck are that it temporarily off balances the opponent, shocks the brain and the resultant hyperextension exposes the throat, larynx and underside of the mandible (jaw) to further strikes (*see* Fig 22).

Checklist

- Formed by pulling the elbow sharply in and downwards, as the wrist travels back along the centreline.
- The angle of the forearm in Man Geng Sau is practically the same as in Tan Sau.
- The elbow must be pulled in, close to the centreline.

- The hand should be positioned with the palm facing inwards, fingers parallel to the ground.
- The elbow should be approximately one fist's distance from the body.
- Always use Man Geng Sau in conjunction with stepping or turning footwork.
- Maintain a vertical posture; do not lean forward.
- The centre of the palm should be on the centreline.
- The forearm and hand should remain relaxed until the Man Geng Sau is applied.

Kwun Sau

Kwun – Cantonese term meaning **rotating.**
Sau – Cantonese term meaning **hand** or
arm.

Kwun Sau is a complex, two-handed defensive structure designed to give maximum body cover in order to gain useful and informative contact with an opponent's attack (*see* Fig 26). At first it can appear to be simply a combination of Tan Sau and Dai Bong Sau to create a < shape, which gives a greater field of cover. However, the ways these structures and their energies are utilized in this combination are quite different and unique.

Kwun Sau can use either or both arms to intercept a strike, and uses a turning stance (Juen Ma) or a stepping stance (Biu Ma) to dissipate the effects of the strike and redirect its force.

Checklist

- Maintain a vertical posture; do not lean forwards or backwards.
- Both elbows should be about the same height, slightly overlapping.
- A combination of a Tan Sau and Dai Bong Sau to create a < shape.
- Both arms drive forwards from the elbows in conjunction with the turning stance.
- Energy is used along the entire arm, fingers and wrists in the Dai Bong Sau.
- The elbows should be on, or just outside the line of the shoulders.
- Lift at the elbows, forwarding energy in the forearms and hands.
- Both wrists should be on the Wing Chun practitioner's centreline

Kau Sau

Kau – Cantonese term meaning **scooping.**
Sau – Cantonese term meaning **hand** or **arm.**

Kau Sau is visually and structurally similar to a Bong Sau in shape, but contacts and controls the opponent's strike using the heel of the palm (*see* Fig 64). It can be deployed when an opponent tries to force a Wing Chun practitioner's arm off the centreline (Gil Sau), to roll over and around their arm and to redirect the force and momentum of their attack.

Checklist

- Formed by rotating the forearm and lifting the elbow.
- The elbow must be higher than the wrist.
- The wrist must be further forward than the elbow.
- The centre of the wrist joint should be on the centreline.
- Maintain a vertical posture; do not lean forwards or backwards.
- Energy is used along the entire arm, fingers and wrist.

Section 1: Moves 1–10

1. Left Biu Sau, right Wu Sau.
2. Forty-five-degree Juen Ma; left Lap Sau, right Man Geng Sau.
3. Right Bong Sau, left Wu Sau.
4. Step 45 degrees, right Tan Sau, left mid Wan Jeung.
5. Step back Seung Gang Sau at approximately 45 degrees to Dummy.
6. Step Biu Ma, Kwun Sau.
7. Step 45 degrees, left Tan Sau, right Wan Jeung.
8. Step back Seung Gang Sau at approximately 45 degrees to Dummy.
9. Face Dummy, left Jum Sau, right Kao Sau.
10. Left Jut Sau, right Jic Jeung.

Fig 21 Left Biu Sau, right Wu Sau.

Fig 22 Forty-five-degree Juen Ma; left Lap Sau, right Man Geng Sau.

Fig 23 Right Bong Sau, left Wu Sau.

Fig 24 Step 45 degrees, right Tan Sau, left mid Wan Jeung.

Fig 25 Step back Seung Gang Sau at approximately 45 degrees to Dummy.

Fig 26 Step Biu Ma, Kwun Sau.

1. Biu Sau

The Dummy form begins with two Biu Sau moves; the first with the left arm thrust upwards along the centreline until the forearm (approximately half-way along the extensor carpi ulnaris and extensor digitorum muscles) makes contact with the Dummy's arm (*see* Fig 21), which in this instance represents

CLOCKWISE FROM TOP LEFT:
Fig 27   Step 45 degrees, left Tan Sau, right Wan Jeung.
Fig 28   Step back Seung Gang Sau at approximately 45 degrees to Dummy.
Fig 29   Face Dummy, left Jum Sau, right Kao Sau.
Fig 30   Left Jut Sau, right Jic Jeung.

the outside of an opponent's left forearm (*see* Fig 32). Upon contact, the Biu Sau maintains that contact, applying and continuing forward pressure from the elbow towards the Dummy's centreline via the Dummy's arms. The Biu Sau then quickly converts to a Lap Sau in conjunction with a 45-degree turn as the second Biu Sau thrusts upwards along the centreline towards the Dummy's trunk (*see* Fig 33).

2. Man Geng Sau

Since the second Biu Sau is not 'intercepted', it instantly converts into a strike, often defined as Man Geng Sau (Fig 22). There are actually three fundamental interpretations or applications of this technique within the Dummy form. The first, and the one usually taught and practised, is Man Geng Sau or neck pulling hand (*see* description above). This is a sharp, jerking in and downward impact to the

CLOCKWISE FROM TOP LEFT:
Fig 31   On guard facing partner.
Fig 32   Left Biu Sau on partner's left punch.
Fig 33   Left Lap Sau, right Biu on centreline.
Fig 34   Right Biu misses.
Fig 35   Right Man Geng Sau and left elbow strike to face/throat.

back of the 'neck' (*see* Fig 22), which can be utilized if the Biu Sau application misses and then overshoots its target (*see* Fig 34).

Alternatively, the Biu Sau can convert to a Wan Jeung (side palm strike) to the jaw/cheek bone of an opponent, driving it back and in to the skull (*see* Fig 37). Depending upon the severity of the self-defence scenario, the thumb can then be thrust into the eye socket (*see* Fig 38).

Another application of this move is a side palm strike over the ear (*see* Fig 39); this creates a concussive trauma, which resembles barotraumas in that there is an extremely

rapid change in pressure against the tympanic membrane (eardrum). This can cause perforation or a rupture of the eardrum, tinnitus, and disorientation and hearing loss, in addition to severe pain.

Man Geng Sau does not appear specifically within the empty hand forms of Wing Chun. However, it utilizes the Jut Sau elbow energy and the structure of Fook Sau as practised in Siu Nim Tao. The advantage of practising this technique on the Dummy is that it tests and ensures that the practitioner's stance is balanced and strong. Because the Dummy is either fixed to or supported on a solid frame

CLOCKWISE FROM TOP LEFT:
Fig 36   Biu Sau on
partner's punch.
Fig 37   Lap Sau, side palm
on partner.
Fig 38   Close-up of side
palm and thumb strike
on partner, shown from
reverse angle.
Fig 39   Lap Sau, side palm
to ear on partner.

or base, it will provide enough resistance to off balance the practitioner if there is a weakness in his stance or posture when either a Lap Sau or Man Geng Sau are carried out.

3. Bong Sau/Wu Sau

The actual movement from Man Geng Sau to form the Bong Sau is largely irrelevant in that it has no direct application. However, the path taken to form Bong Sau should be precise in order to initiate a good structure and practise the correct formation of the Bong Sau. The Man Geng Sau arm should be slightly withdrawn, then the forearm

and elbow rotated anticlockwise, bringing the wrist into the Wing Chun practitioner's centreline, and the Bong Sau and the supporting Wu Sau forwarded to make contact on the Dummy's arm. If the distance from the Dummy was measured correctly at the beginning of the form, the Bong Sau structure should be correct – the elbow higher than the wrist and the wrist further forward than the elbow. The relaxed wrist of the Bong Sau arm should make contact at a point within 2in (50mm) of the end of the Dummy's arm, which in this instance represents the outside of an opponent's left wrist.

Fig 40   Close-up of Tan/palm and foot position.

Dummy's leg and repositioning at 45 degrees (*see* Fig 24), is one of the core techniques of the first (and second) section of the Dummy. It is essential that the timing and coordination are correct, so that the Tan Sau, Wan Jeung and foot contact arrive powerfully and simultaneously: *three techniques – one sound.*

> In performing every set and stroke, you must pay attention to have the waist and footing coordinating in exerting force.
>
> *Ip Ching*

Whilst stepping, re-angling and moving around the Dummy, the Bong Sau/Tan Sau must maintain both contact with the Dummy's arm and forward pressure along it, towards the body of the Dummy. The weight must be placed over the left leg and the hips angled to face the Dummy before the Tan Sau, Wan Jeung and leg are driven forward. If the footwork is correct, the practitioner will be in the best possible position to apply the hand and leg techniques powerfully. If the body position is correct, the practitioner will have three points of contact on the Dummy (*see* Figs 24 and 40):

It is important not to overturn the body; the Bong Sau elbow must be positioned further away from the Dummy's body than the end of the Dummy's arms. If the elbow is closer than the end of the Dummy's arms, the arm cannot be smoothly rotated and maintain contact when rolling to Tan Sau, instead it will need to be retracted slightly to clear the end of the Dummy's arm.

The Wu Sau should be positioned half-way between the practitioner's wrist and his nose, with the base of the palm approximately the same height as the Bong Sau elbow (*see* Fig 23).

4. Tan Sau/Wan Jeung

The Bong Sau to Tan Sau/Wan Jeung movement, in conjunction with stepping around the

1. The right Tan Sau wrist on the end of the Dummy's arm.
2. The left palm strike to the centreline of the Dummy trunk.
3. The right ankle against the Dummy's leg

If the distance is incorrect, the palm strike will not reach; if the angle is incorrect, then either the Tan Sau or the side palm will not make contact correctly; and if the distance around the Dummy is not correct, the ankle will not be touching the Dummy's leg. Only one position can be correct; this is one of the great benefits of Wooden Dummy training.

The Tan Sau makes contact and controls the Dummy's arm with the outside edge of the forearm between the wrist and mid

CLOCKWISE FROM TOP LEFT:
Fig 41　On guard facing partner.
Fig 42　Bong Sau on outside gate of punch.
Fig 43　Bong Sau to Tan half move.
Fig 44　Tan Da with foot on inside gate.

point along the radius and the brachioradialis muscle. The elbow joint is 'fixed' using elbow energy; the palm and fingers should be relaxed and the thumb tucked in and over the palm, but not actually touching the palm, which would constrict the pressure point Li 4 (He Gu point) and restrict energy flow along the large intestine meridian.

In application, the Bong Sau contacts on the outside (outside gate) of an opponent's arm (*see* Fig 42). Should the opponent push or force the Wing Chun practitioner's arm outwards away from the centreline, the Bong Sau can quickly convert into an inside gate Tan Sau with a simultaneous strike, whilst stepping into the centreline (*see* Fig 44) in accordance with the Wing Chun maxim: *Lin Siu Dai Da* – simultaneous attack and defence.

Alternatively, the Bong Sau can contact on the inside of an opponent's arm (inside gate), referred to as wrong Bong Sau or Bong Chor Sau (*see* Fig 46). As the punch would most likely be curving inwards (human anatomy dictates that the most powerful and natural punches curve inwards, pivoting around the spine, turning the hips and shoulders), the Bong Chor Sau can swiftly be converted into a Tan Sau by using a quick turning stance (Juen Ma), sharply dropping

CLOCKWISE FROM TOP LEFT:
Fig 45   On guard facing partner.
Fig 46   Inside Bong Sau to partner's punch.
Fig 47   Bong Sau to Tan half move.
Fig 48   Tan Da completed on partner with foot contact.

the elbow whilst rotating and maintaining contact at the wrist. Tan Sau is always used in combination with a strike, which on the Dummy and in the example shown is a mid-level side palm strike (Wan Jeung) to the false or to the floating ribs. The side palm should contact and drive in the energy to the centre of the Dummy using the base of the palm. At the same time the side of the Wing Chun practitioner's foot makes and maintains contact with the opponent's foot (*see* Fig 48). The advantage of the foot contact is that if the attacker steps back, lifts their foot to kick or tries to step, the

movement can be felt instantly via that contact and responded to immediately and efficiently.

5. Seung Gang Sau

The next movement is to reposition into a neutral stance (50:50 weight distribution) at approximately a 45-degree angle to the Dummy with Seung Gang Sau (*see* Fig 25). The upper Gang Sau arm drives forward from the elbow to make contact with the Dummy's arm with the inner/upper part of the forearm, about half-way along the ulna and the flexor carpi ulnaris muscle, with the

CLOCKWISE FROM TOP LEFT:
Fig 49 On guard facing partner.
Fig 50 Opponent fakes a right punch.
Fig 51 Double Gang at 45 degrees to counter a front thrust kick.
Fig 52 Opponent throws another punch; counter Kwun/Biu Ma.

elbow pulled in close to the practitioner's centreline. Simultaneously, the lower Gang Sau forwards and connects with the lower, centre arm of the Dummy with the heel of the right palm. The low Gang Sau is similar in shape and structure to the Dai Bong Sau practised in Chum Kiu. If the body position is correct when stepping with the double Gang Sau, then both arms will be in contact with the Dummy's arms with the correct vertical body posture, shoulders relaxed and a strong neutral stance.

It is often thought that this technique and the Kwun Sau that follows it in the Dummy form are used to cover a double punch. However, that would not be practical, nor in reality likely, in the street.

Gang Sau and Kwun Sau can, however, be used to cover a strike when the height of the attack is undetermined, for example where it appears as if the attacker is about to punch (*see* Fig 50), but then launches a kick instead (*see* Fig 51). Seung Gang Sau can be used to cover a larger area and can cover a potential punch or kick. In the example above, Kwun Sau is applied to step in and control the next punch.

47

Fig 53   On guard facing partner.
Fig 54   Opponent throws a left punch; defend left Biu Sau.
Fig 55   Opponent grabs the punch, pulls and throws another punch.
Fig 56   Counter opponents punch with Biu Ma step and Kwun Sau.

6. Kwun Sau

Rolling into the Kwun Sau technique is carried out in conjunction with a short Biu Ma step parallel to the frame of the Dummy. It is important not to retract the arms from the Dummy's arms any more than is necessary to roll into the Kwun Sau structure – do not retract for 'power'. As both hands make contact on the Dummy, the energy should be driven into the centre of the Dummy's body (*see* Fig 26). As discussed above in relation to Seung Gang Sau, Kwun Sau may be used to

cover a strike when the height of the attack is vague or unresolved. In a combat application it is possible that one, but not both hands are in contact with the opponent's hands (*see* Figs 52 and 56).

When stepping from Seung Gang Sau to Kwun Sau, it is quite common to 'overstep' and therefore compromise the Kwun Sau structure. To form the Kwun Sau the correct body position is where the right hip is in front of the centre of the Dummy (easily measured by using the low, centre Dummy's arm). The

CLOCKWISE FROM TOP LEFT:
Fig 57   On guard facing partner.
Fig 58   Opponent punches; counter Bong Sau.
Fig 59   Opponent punches again. Step around with Tan Sau (half move shown).
Fig 60   Step in with Tan Da and contact on to opponent's foot.

correct position can be checked by standing in a neutral stance in front of the Dummy and then turning (Juen Ma) to approximately 45 degrees to the Dummy, sitting the majority of the body mass on to the left leg.

7. Tan Sau/Wan Jeung

The Kwun Sau to Tan Sau/Wan Jeung movement, in conjunction with stepping around the Dummy's leg and repositioning at 45 degrees, is part of the core techniques of the first and second sections of the Wooden Dummy. As mentioned previously, it is essential that the timing and coordination are correct so that the Tan Sau, Wan Jeung and foot contact arrive at the same time. The difference between this technique and the previous Tan Sau application, and the key to this particular movement, is that whilst stepping, re-angling and moving around the Dummy, the Dai Bong Sau disengages from the middle low arm and quickly re-engages contact with the Dummy's upper arm to form Tan Sau (*see* Fig 27). The disengaging

CLOCKWISE FROM TOP LEFT:
Fig 61   On guard facing opponent.
Fig 62   Opponent punches; counter Tan Da.
Fig 63   Opponent punches again; counter Seung Gang Sau.
Fig 64   Immediately turn with Kau Sau and side palm strike.

and rapid re-engaging of contact is the key to this sequence; it should be done with the minimal amount of movement and without actually withdrawing the hands and then impacting hard to regain contact. As soon as the Tan Sau makes light contact with the Dummy's arm, it should apply forward pressure along that arm towards the body of the Dummy. As stated previously, if the footwork is correct then the practitioner will be in the best possible position to apply the hand and leg techniques powerfully.

In application, this sequence of disengaging and re-engaging contact could be used against an attacker's one or two punch combination (*see* Figs 58–60). For example, the opponent throws a left punch, which can easily be intercepted by a right Bong Sau (*see* Fig 58). If the opponent quickly throws a second (left) punch, the Wing Chun practitioner can easily take a short Bui Ma step, turn and step in with Tan Da, controlling the opponent's foot with their own (*see* Fig 60).

CLOCKWISE FROM TOP LEFT:
Fig 65   On guard facing opponent.
Fig 66   Opponent punches; counter Juen Ma/Seung Gang Sau.
Fig 67   Turn and counter with Kau Sau/Jum Sau.
Fig 68   Continue; Biu Ma, Jut Sau and centreline control.
Fig 69   Jut Sau and Jic Jeung.

8. Seung Gang Sau

The Seung Gang Sau this side of the Dummy is a mirrored repeat of the previous Seung Gang Sau (*see* Fig 28).

9. Kau Sau/Jum Sau

From the Gang Sau (*see* Fig 28), step to face the Dummy in a neutral stance, maintaining contact with the high Gang Sau and then circling counter-clockwise to form Kau Sau. This movement is similar to a Bong Sau in shape but with contact on the heel of the palm (*see* Fig 29). The step and the hip turn together to create a short, sharp retraction as the Kau Sau forms; at the same time the low Gang Sau cuts upwards.

In application, the low Gang Sau would probably cut up the centreline and strike the opponent. However, on the Dummy the low Gang Sau travels up the centreline towards the Dummy's 'head' but is 'intercepted' by the Dummy's arm and therefore converts into Jum Sau on to the outside of the left Dummy arm. The Jum Sau contacts with the inner/upper part of the forearm, about half-way along the ulna and the flexor carpi ulnaris muscle, with the hand and arm rotated inwards so that the forearm and elbow are pulled in and down close to the practitioner's centreline, covering the mid-section of the torso (*see* Fig 29). Upon contact, Fa Ging energy is used to form the Jum Sau. Immediately, the energy is switched off and replaced by forward elbow energy, sufficient to maintain the necessary structural integrity.

10. Jut Sau/Jic Jeung

As soon as the left Jum Sau makes contact with the Dummy's arm, it switches to Jut Sau; the Kau Sau elbow quickly drops into the centreline and the arm drives up and along the centreline to strike with Jic Jeung (*see* Fig 30).

The vertical palm strike is the weapon of choice in this instance because its structure dictates that the elbow is positioned slightly off the centreline and can be used to contact and control the Dummy's arm (or an opponent's punch; *see* Fig 68) prior to the palm strike landing. The palm strike should remain relaxed until the fingertips touch the Dummy, then the heel of the palm should be snapped forwards, driven inwards upon contact and immediately relaxed afterwards. This results in a driven energy from contact, rather than a hit, applying energy into, not on to, the Dummy. As the Dummy rocks on its frame due to the energy of the palm strike, the fingertips should remain in contact with the Dummy's body, monitoring its movement as the amplitude diminishes.

In application, the vertical palm strike is usually aimed at the nose, resulting in a nasal fracture, or to the jaw, resulting in a displaced or fractured mandible, commonly referred to as a broken jaw (*see* Fig 69). The strike is carried out using the heel of the palm, in effect striking with the end of the ulna and

radius bones. The relaxed fingertips make the initial contact, and then the palm snaps forward at the wrist into the target, immediately relaxing again afterwards.

Gum Sau, Jic Jeung and Wan Jeung all make contact/strike using the heel of the palm. The actual contact is on the carpals (eight small wrist bones), which transmit the resultant force through, and are supported by, the two forearm bones – the ulna and the radius. It is vital to always contact and strike with the heel of the palm in order to avoid a sprained wrist or similar personal injury.

Section 2: Moves 11–20

The second section of the Dummy form is a mirrored repeat of the first section, beginning with a right Biu Sau (*see* Figs 70–79). The only variation is that the last movement is a side palm (Wan Jeung) and is applied at the mid-level, rather than the high level, vertical palm (Jic Jeung).

The Wan Jeung side palm is used when striking beneath a high punch or against a taller opponent. The side palm utilizes the same relaxed energy as the vertical palm, only snapping the wrist forwards as the fingertips make contact, applying energy into rather than hitting the surface of the Dummy or opponent. In application, the side palm usually aims to the floating ribs (the last two pairs of ribs that only attach to the spine), causing fractures, flail chest or even a pneumothorax (punctured/collapsed lung).

11. Right Biu Sau, left Wu Sau.
12. 45-degree Juen Ma, right Lap Sau, left Man Geng Sau.
13. Left Bong Sau, right Wu Sau.
14. Step 45 degrees, left Tan Sau, right mid Wan Jeung.
15. Step back Seung Gang Sau at approximately 45 degrees to Dummy.
16. Biu Ma with Kwun Sau.

Fig 70 Right Biu Sau, left Wu Sau.

Fig 71 45-degree Juen Ma, right Lap Sau, left Man Geng Sau.

Fig 72 Left Bong Sau, right Wu Sau.

Fig 73 Step 45 degrees, left Tan Sau, right mid Wan Jeung.

Fig 74 Step back Seung Gang Sau at approximately 45 degrees to Dummy.

Fig 75 Biu Ma with Kwun Sau.

17. Step 45 degrees, right Tan Sau, left mid Wan Jeung.
18. Step back Seung Gang Sau at approximately 45 degrees to Dummy.
19. Face Dummy, right Jum Sau, left Kao Sau.
20. Right Jut Sau, left mid Wan Jeung.

CLOCKWISE FROM TOP LEFT:
Fig 76   Step 45 degrees, right Tan Sau, left mid Wan Jeung.
Fig 77   Step back Seung Gang Sau at approximately 45 degrees to Dummy.
Fig 78   Face Dummy, right Jum Sau, left Kao Sau.
Fig 79   Right Jut Sau, left mid Wan Jeung.

Section 3

This section introduces a further new technique – Wan Gerk – sometimes called Wan Tek.

Wan Gerk
Wan – Cantonese term meaning **side**.
Gerk – Cantonese term meaning **kick** *n.*, either of the two lower limbs.

Wan Gerk is a low 'side' kick, used to stamp into an opponent's knee, shin or thigh.

It is critical when kicking that the body's mass is fully supported on the one leg prior to the other leg leaving the ground. This is essential to avoid visually telegraphing the kick following the Wing Chun principle, *Mo Ying Gerk* – shadowless kick (literally no shadow kick), sometimes referred to as 'invisible kick', because the kick is very difficult to read due to the lack of, or minimal, body movement when kicking. However, when applying Wan Gerk, the body has to lean back slightly for several reasons.

The first reason is to avoid putting all the flex and stress on the hip joint of the kicking leg. Secondly, if the torso is vertical, when the kick lands on the opponent's lead knee joint, the attacker's momentum may cause them to fall forward and they may land an opportune strike. Leaning back means any strike thrown by the opponent, whether accidental or deliberate, is intercepted by the Wing Chun practitioner's hands, not 'blocked' by the face. Finally, in order to generate a more powerful kick, leaning slightly lines up the spinal column, tilts the hips perpendicular to the spine and creates a direct line of force through them down to the heel of the striking foot (*see* Fig 112).

When applying the sidekick, the ball of the relaxed foot makes contact first, then upon that contact the heel snaps forward to apply the striking force, in a similar action to the way that a palm strike makes light contact, and then snaps the wrist energy forwards into the Dummy. Wan Gerk can be used to intercept an opponent at low level – a stamp to the shin. This uses the principle of Jeet Tek (intercepting leg) to initiate contact whilst keeping them at a controlling range.

Checklist

- The body's mass must be fully supported on the one leg prior to the kick leaving the ground.
- When applying Wan Gerk the body has to lean back slightly.
- The ball of the relaxed foot makes contact first then, upon that contact, the heel snaps forward.
- Wan Gerk should be used with a simultaneous hand defence – Bong Sau/Wu Sau.

- The kick should be performed similar to a stamping action, driving the heel down on to the target.
- Wan Gerk is often applied to an opponent's knee or shin.
- Wan Gerk can be used to intercept and gain the initial contact at low level with an opponent.

Section 3: Moves 21–38

21. Right Pak Sau, left Wu Sau.
22. Left Pak Sau, right Wu Sau.
23. Right Pak Sau, left Wu Sau.
24. 45-degree Juen Ma, left Pak Sau, right Wu Sau.
25. Left Fak Sau, right Wu Sau.
26. Face Dummy with left Gum Sau, right mid-level Jic Kuen.
27. 45-degree Juen Ma, right Pak Sau, left Wu Sau.
28. Right Fak Sau with Wu Sau.
29. Face Dummy with right Gum Sau, left mid-level Jic Kuen.
30. 45-degree Juen Ma, right Dai Bong Sau, left Wu Sau.
31. Step at 45 degrees past and then in to Dummy, with right Fak Sau, left Pak Sau.
32. Right Wan Gerk; right Bong Sau, left Wu Sau.
33. Step back in front of Dummy, at 45 degrees Juen Ma, left Dai Bong Sau, right Wu Sau.
34. Step 45 degrees past and then in to Dummy, with right Pak Sau, left Fak Sau.
35. Left Wan Gerk with left Bong Sau, right Wu Sau.
36. Step back Seung Gang Sau at approximately 45 degrees to Dummy.
37. Face Dummy, right Kao Sau, left Jum Sau.
38. Left Jut Sau, right Jic Jeung.

Fig 80   Right Pak Sau, left Wu Sau.

Fig 81   Left Pak Sau, right Wu Sau.

Fig 82   Right Pak Sau, left Wu Sau.

Fig 83   45-degree Juen Ma, left Pak Sau, right Wu Sau.

Fig 84   Left Fak Sau, right Wu Sau.

Fig 85   Face Dummy with left Gum Sau, right mid-level Jic Kuen.

21. **Right Pak Sau/Wu Sau**

Upon completion of the right Jut Sau in the previous section, both arms should simply drop into the centreline (right arm lead) and then perform a right Pak Sau with a left Wu Sau, without a turning stance (*see* Fig 80).

In application, Pak Sau is always used in conjunction with a turning stance (Juen

Fig 86 45-degree Juen Ma, right Pak Sau, left Wu Sau.

Fig 87 Right Fak Sau with Wu Sau.

Fig 88 Face Dummy with right Gum Sau, left mid-level Jic Kuen.

Fig 89 45-degree Juen Ma, right Dai Bong Sau, left Wu Sau.

Fig 90 Step at 45 degrees past and then in to Dummy, with right Fak Sau, left Pak Sau.

Fig 91 Right Wan Gerk; right Bong Sau, left Wu Sau.

Ma) to avoid the strike and to give greater power to the Pak Sau. However, a turning stance is not required when applying Pak Sau on the Dummy as the arms are already angled away from the Wing Chun practitioner.

The Pak Sau, which must be correctly structured, as per Siu Nim Tao, should be

57

Fig 92 Step back in front of Dummy, at 45 degrees Juen Ma, left Dai Bong Sau, right Wu Sau.

Fig 93 Step 45 degrees past and then in to Dummy, with right Pak Sau, left Fak Sau.

Fig 94 Left Wan Gerk with left Bong Sau, right Wu Sau.

Fig 95 Step back Seung Gang Sau at approximately 45 degrees to Dummy.

Fig 96 Face Dummy, right Kao Sau, left Jum Sau.

Fig 97 Left Jut Sau, right Jic Jeung.

driven 45 degrees forwards and away from the body into the Dummy's arm, which in turn directs the force into the Dummy's body. The centre of the heel of the Pak Sau palm (in essence the end of the radius and ulna bones) should make sharp contact with the last 1–2in (25–50mm) of the Dummy's arm, which now represents the outside of

Fig 98   On guard facing
opponent.

Fig 99   Opponent punches;
counter Juen Ma, Pak Sau/Wu
Sau.

Fig 100   Pak Sau energy into
opponent's centreline causes
loss of balance and structure.

an opponent's left elbow. The fingers should be vertical and straight, but not tensed; the thumb should be locked, bent over, but not touching the palm. The palm should be parallel to the angle of the Dummy's arm, and the wrist should remain relaxed until just prior to contact on the Dummy's arm. A short, sharp energy (Fa Ging) is then used to lock the wrist and drive forward the centre of the heel of the palm to apply some energy into, but not beyond, the Dummy's arm. Immediately after contact is made and the energy is applied, the Pak Sau should be relaxed whilst maintaining contact with the Dummy's arm. A left Wu Sau, which should be high enough to protect the practitioner's throat, supports the Pak Sau.

In application, a turning stance (Juen Ma) is used to turn and avoid an opponent's attack, take up a safe and powerful position, and generate a short, sharp rotational force, accelerating and adding power to the Pak Sau (*see* Fig 99). The Pak Sau is applied to the outside of an opponent's arm, just below, but close to, the elbow joint. This not only

controls the opponent's arm, it also applies a force into the opponent's stance, which in turn causes a temporary loss of posture and balance (*see* Fig 100).

An additional benefit of controlling the opponent's elbow is that it can prohibit their ability to twist their body sharply and counter punch with their opposite arm. The Pak Sau applies a small amount of pressure into the opponent's centreline and towards their opposite shoulder and, by the application of a sharp burst of energy should the opponent try to turn it, the opponent is unable to twist their upper body to bring the other arm into play.

The Pak Sau is supported structurally by Wu Sau and provides protective cover to the practitioner's throat and neck whilst acting as a back-up cover should the Pak Sau miss its intended contact point or not intercept the strike. In addition, the Wu Sau is ideally placed to be able to travel forwards and either diagonally upwards or downwards to intercept any second strike, or, if necessary, it can be driven forward as a strike.

For detailed information about the triangular structure of Wing Chun techniques, see my first book, *Simply … Wing Chun Kung Fu*.

22. Left Pak Sau/Wu Sau

As soon as the right Pak Sau has completed, the right hand drops slightly, giving clear access for the left Wu Sau to drive directly forward as a left Pak Sau to the opposite Dummy's arm, which again represents the outside of an opponent's arm. Simultaneously, the right arm retracts beneath the left arm to form a Wu Sau, which covers and protects the practitioner's throat area (*see* Fig 81). This Pak Sau/Wu Sau combination on the Dummy is again implemented without a turning stance.

23. Right Pak Sau/Wu Sau

This is a repeat of move 21 (*see* Fig 82).

It is often believed, quite incorrectly, that the sequence of three Pak Sau movements is used to parry a series of jabs or successive straight punches. However, in reality, each Pak Sau/Wu Sau movement should be considered and practised in isolation, although it is possible to use them in combination if the situation dictates it to be necessary.

24. Left Pak Sau/Wu Sau with Juen Ma

Mechanically, this Pak Sau/Wu Sau combination is the same as the previous Pak Sau combinations, except this time it is used with a 45-degree Juen Ma turn. Whereas the first three Pak Sau movements drive forwards at an approximate 45-degree angle to intercept the Dummy's arm, this Pak Sau pulls in slightly upon contact, as if trying to pass the 'punch' past the practitioner's right shoulder (*see* Fig 83). It is important not to overturn the body when applying the Pak Sau; the wrist should remain closer to the Dummy's body than the elbow so that the Fak Sau can be driven from the elbow into the Dummy's

body. If the body overturns, then the elbow will be too far forward – almost a Lan Sau position – and the Fak Sau will take a circular line, pivoting at the elbow, rather than a linear path, and will be inefficient and much less powerful.

25. Left Fak Sau, Right Wu Sau

As soon as the left Pak Sau makes contact with the Dummy's arm, it relaxes and immediately drives forward to the Dummy's 'neck' as a Fak Sau. The hand remains relaxed as the Fak Sau travels towards the Dummy, snapping energy forward through the edge of the wrist into the Dummy's body upon contact (*see* Fig 84). The Fak Sau primarily aims into the throat area and the larynx or slightly upwards to beneath the mandible (jawbone), although it can be used to strike into the face.

26. Left Gum Sau, Right Punch

Turn to face the Dummy with a left Gum Sau and a right mid-level punch (*see* Fig 85). The Fak Sau drops sharply inwards and downwards to drop on to the end of the Dummy's arm as a Gum Sau, the elbow of which is down at an approximate 45-degree angle. At the same time, the Wu Sau drives forward as a mid-level punch, except that the punch does not actually strike the Dummy; it stops upon contact to avoid unnecessary injury to the hand.

There has always been debate as to whether the left-hand technique should be a Gum Sau or a Jut Sau. It is difficult to say that it should be one, rather than the other, because they can both be applied on the Dummy and in application: Jut Sau is considered neither a specific technique nor a structure, but more an application of energy. It is a short, sharp jerking action downwards and inwards towards waist level and can be carried out using the heel of the palm or the palm of the hand, which is dragged sharply inwards by

CLOCKWISE FROM TOP LEFT:
Fig 109   On guard facing partner.
Fig 110   Opponent punches; counter Dai Bong Sau/Wu Sau.
Fig 111   Opponent throws a second punch; counter Biu Ma, Fak Sau with Pak Sau and control the opponent's foot.
Fig 112   Wan Gerk to opponent's knee, cover Bong Sau/Wu Sau.
Fig 113   Follow Pak Sau/ punch and Biu Ma into the centreline.

the body almost in front of the Dummy, angled at approximately 45 degrees with a low left Bong Sau and a high right Wu Sau to cover and protect the throat area (*see* Fig 92).

As before (*see* movement 30), the Dai Bong Sau, as the forearm contacts the Dummy's arm, rotates inwards to ensure that the force upon contact is directed into the Dummy, not across the Dummy's arm.

34. Left Fak Sau, Right Pak Sau with 45-Degree Step In

This is a mirror repeat of movement 31 (*see* Fig 93).

35. Right Wan Gerk, Right Bong Sau and Left Wu Sau

This is a mirror repeat of movement 32 (*see* Fig 94).

CLOCKWISE FROM TOP LEFT:
Fig 114   On guard facing opponent.
Fig 115   Opponent punches; counter Wan Gerk to knee.
Fig 116   Opponent throws second punch; counter Juen Ma, Seung Gang Sau.
Fig 117   Opponent throws another punch; counter Juen Ma, Kau Sau/Jic Kuen.
Fig 118   Biu Ma in; Lan Sau/Chair Pie.

36. Seung Gang Sau

As soon as the Wan Gerk is delivered, the foot is quickly put down on the floor in conjunction with a small Biu Ma step to position the body into a neutral stance (50:50 weight distribution) at approximately a 45-degree angle to the Dummy with Seung Gang Sau (*see* Fig 95). As discussed previously, the high right Gang Sau arm drives forward to make contact with the Dummy's arm with the inner/upper part of the forearm, the elbow pulled in close to the practitioner's centreline. Simultaneously, the lower left Gang Sau forwards and connects with the lower, centre arm of the Dummy with the heel of the right palm.

In application, the Seung Gang Sau can be applied to provide body cover as the Wan Gerk kicking leg is returned to the floor (*see* Fig 116). In the example shown, Seung Gang Sau is applied to receive and defend against a second punch. Due to the speed of the second punch, it is not possible to step to a neutral stance, so the Seung Gang Sau is used in conjunction with Juen Ma. Should the opponent throw a further punch, Juen Ma can be quickly and easily utilized to avoid the strike and Kau Sau can be used to 'collect' and control the punch whilst simultaneously counter-striking with a punch to the face (*see* Fig 117). It is then possible to quickly Biu Ma in, closing the opponent down and controlling the opponent's arms with Lan Sau whilst simultaneously striking with Chair Pie (diagonal elbow strike) (*see* Fig 118).

37. Face Dummy, Right Kau Sau, Left Jum Sau

From the Gang Sau, step to face the Dummy in a neutral stance, maintaining contact with the high Gang Sau and circling counterclockwise to form Kau Sau, as described previously.

The step and the hip turn together to create a short, sharp retraction as the Kau Sau forms, and at the same time the low Gang Sau cuts upwards and up the centreline towards the 'head' of the Dummy. Since the Dummy's arms are fixed in position, the left arm is 'intercepted' by the Dummy's arm and therefore converts into Jum Sau on to the outside of the Dummy's arm, contacting with the inner/upper part of the forearm (*see* Fig 96).

38. Left Jut Sau, Right Jic Jeung

As soon as the left Jum Sau makes contact with the Dummy's arm, it switches to Jut Sau; the Kau Sau quickly drops into the centreline and drives up the centreline to strike with Jic Jeung. As detailed earlier, the vertical palm strike keeps the elbow slightly off the centreline to maintain contact and control the Dummy's arm (or in application the opponent's punch) prior to the palm strike landing (*see* Fig 97). As described in the previous section (*see* movement 10), the palm strike should remain relaxed until the fingertips touch the Dummy, then the palm

should be snapped forwards, driven inwards upon contact, and immediately relaxed afterwards.

Section 4: Moves 39–57

39. Seung Jum Sau.
40. Seung Huen Sau.
41. Seung Dai Wan Jeung.
42. Seung Tan Sau.
43. Seung Ha Wan Jeung.
44. Seung Jut Sau.
45. 45-degree Juen Ma, left Kao Sau, right Jum Sau.
46. 45-degree Juen Ma, right Kao Sau, left Jum Sau.
47. Face Dummy with left Jut Sau, right Jic Jeung.
48 45-degree Juen Ma, right Bong Sau, left Wu Sau.
49. Step left at 45 degrees, Juen Ma, right Tan Sau, left Wan Jeung and right Jic Gerk.
50. Step back, Seung Gang Sau at approximately 45 degrees to Dummy.
51. Face Dummy with left Kao Sau, right Jum Sau.
52. Right Gum Sau, left mid Wan Jeung.
53. Turn left at 45 degrees with left Bong Sau, right Wu Sau.
54. Step right at 45 degrees, Juen Ma, left Tan Sau, right mid-level Wan Jeung, left Jic Gerk.
55. Step back Seung Gang Sau at approximately 45 degrees to Dummy.
56. Face Dummy, right Kao Sau, left Jum Sau.
57. Left Jut Sau, right Jic Jeung.

39. Seung Jum Sau

Drive the double Jum Sau up and forwards to make contact on the outside of both the Dummy's arms with the inside edge of the forearms, whilst rolling the elbows and forearms inwards and forwards. The arms should

Fig 119   Seung Jum Sau.

Fig 120   Seung Huen Sau.

Fig 121   Seung Dai Wan Jeung.

Fig 122   Seung Tan Sau.

Fig 123   Seung Ha Wan Jeung.

Fig 124   Seung Jut Sau.

be parallel to each other and the palms horizontal (*see* Fig 119). Once contact is made, maintain a forward energy from the elbows towards the Dummy.

40. Seung Huen Sau

Maintain contact with the Dummy's arms whilst slowly and powerfully circling the wrists inwards, over and between

Fig 125 45-degree Juen Ma, left Kao Sau, right Jum Sau.

Fig 126 45-degree Juen Ma, right Kao Sau, left Jum Sau.

Fig 127 Face Dummy with left Jut Sau, right Jic Jeung.

Fig 128 45-degree Juen Ma, right Bong Sau, left Wu Sau.

Fig 129 Step left at 45 degrees, Juen Ma, right Tan Sau, left Wan Jeung and right Jic Gerk.

Fig 130 Step back, Seung Gang Sau at approximately 45 degrees to Dummy.

the Dummy's arms. When it is not possible to rotate the wrists any more without the elbows drifting outwards, slip the forearms in between the Dummy's arms (still maintaining contact) and continue the wrist rotation until the relaxed palms face the Dummy (*see* Fig 120).

69

CLOCKWISE FROM TOP LEFT:
Fig 131   Face Dummy with left Kao Sau, right Jum Sau.
Fig 132   Right Gum Sau, left mid Wan Jeung.
Fig 133   Turn left at 45 degrees with left Bong Sau, right Wu Sau.
Fig 134   Step right at 45 degrees, Juen Ma, left Tan Sau, right mid-level Wan Jeung, left Jic Gerk.
Fig 135   Step back Seung Gang Sau at approximately 45 degrees to Dummy.

41. Seung Dai Wan Jeung

As soon as the palms face the Dummy, thrust both arms forward until the finger-tips make contact with the Dummy's body, and then press the palms forward to make light contact on the Dummy's body. Upon that contact, drive a short, sharp wrist-snap energy into the Dummy (*see* Fig 121), immediately relaxing the wrists, whilst maintaining light fingertip contact with the

Dummy's body as it recoils due to the wrist-snap energy.

In application, it would be impractical and illogical to apply the Jum Sau and Huen Sau using both arms; rather they should predominately be applied using just one arm on to one of the opponent's arms.

For example, as soon as contact is gained with a high Jum Sau to the outside of an opponent's arm (*see* Fig 139), Huen Sau

LEFT: Fig 136 Face Dummy, right Kao Sau, left Jum Sau.
RIGHT: Fig 137 Left Jut Sau, right Jic Jeung.

can be used to quickly circle and cut into the inside gate to attack the centreline, or to cut from the inside gate to the outside gate. Alternatively, as illustrated below, Huen Sau can be used to control both arms when fired in a quick one–two succession (*see* Fig 140), opening up an alternative line of counter-attack (*see* Fig 141).

42. Seung Tan Sau

From the mid-level palm strike, drive both arms up the centreline as a double Tan Sau, contacting the inside of both Dummy's arms with the outside edge of the forearms (*see* Fig 122) between the wrist and mid-point along the radius and the brachioradialis muscle. The elbow joint is 'fixed' using elbow energy, the palm and fingers should be relaxed and the thumb tucked in and over the palm, but not actually touching the palm, which would constrict the pressure point Li 4 (He Gu point) and restrict energy flow along the large intestine meridian.

In application, in accordance with the Wing Chun maxim, *Lin Siu Dai Da* – simultaneous attack and defence, Tan Sau is used at the same time as a strike, possibly a punch, palm strike or even an elbow strike (*see* Fig 146).

43. Seung Ha Wan Jeung

From the Seung Tan Sau position, thrust both arms up and forward towards the Dummy's 'face' until the fingertips make contact on the Dummy, then press the palms forward to make light contact on the Dummy's body. Upon that contact drive a short, sharp wrist-snap energy into the Dummy (*see* Fig 123), immediately relaxing the wrists, whilst maintaining light fingertip contact with the Dummy's body as it recoils due to the wrist-snap energy applied.

When applied in combat, the wrist snap can be used to drive the thumb into the eye socket, if the situation deems it appropriate or necessary (*see* Fig 147).

44. Seung Jut Sau

From the double palm strike, allow the elbows to drift outwards slightly so that they are just outside the upper Dummy's arms, then sharply pull the elbows down and inwards, contacting the outside edge of both

71

CLOCKWISE FROM TOP LEFT:
Fig 138   On guard facing opponent.
Fig 139   Opponent punches; counter Juen Ma, Jum Sau/Wu Sau.
Fig 140   Opponent throws second punch; counter Huen Sau (half move shown).
Fig 141   Huen Sau completed, Biu Man in Wan Jeung/Wu Sau.

Dummy's arms with the inside of the forearms (*see* Fig 124).

As discussed previously, the Wooden Dummy is an excellent tool to provide muscular resistance training since it hardly moves. Applying Seung Jut Sau will develop the triceps, abdominals and the leg muscles (stance).

In application, Jut Sau is a useful tool to combat a strong or tense opponent. When an opponent tenses his or her arms, either to use force or to resist the Wing Chun practitioner's techniques, a short, sharp action, such as Jut Sau, can be applied to use that tension and force against them.

For example, if, upon contact on the outside of an opponent's arm with Jum Sau, the opponent tries to powerfully and quickly pull his arm inwards to off balance the Wing Chun practitioner, Jut Sau can be used to counter that energy and in fact off balance the opponent. As the opponent tries to pull their arm inwards (pulling the wrist towards their body), the Jut Sau uses a short, sharp

Fig 142   On guard facing partner.

Fig 143   Opponent punches; counter Juen Ma, Jum Sau/ Wu Sau.

Fig 144   Opponent throws second punch; counter Huen Sau (half move shown).

Fig 145   Huen Sau completed, Biu Man in Wan Jeung/Wu Sau.

Fig 146   Opponent throws left punch; quickly step back and turn Wan Jeung/Tan Sau.

Fig 147   Juen Ma, Wan Jeung/Wu Sau to face.

jerking energy down and inwards, just sufficient to counter the initial pulling action. This momentarily prevents the opponent's wrist from moving; as a result, the bicep, which is contracting to shorten the distance between the wrist and the shoulder, pulls the opponent forward and off balance.

For a more practical example, once contact is gained, if an opponent tries to force the Wing Chun practitioner's arms away to

CLOCKWISE FROM TOP LEFT:
Fig 148   On guard facing opponent.
Fig 149   Opponent punches; counter Juen Ma, Jum Sau/Wu Sau.
Fig 150   Opponent attempts to push off the centreline to throw a second punch.
Fig 151   Counter Juen Ma, Jut Sau/Wu Sau to control both arms and off balance the opponent.

enable a counter-punch to be thrown, Jut Sau can be used to control the hand already in contact, therefore controlling the second strike (*see* Figs 148–151).

45. 45-Degree Juen Ma; Left Kao Sau, Right Jum Sau

From the double Jut Sau, turn 45 degrees whilst circling the left arm clockwise around the Dummy's arm to form Kao Sau, maintaining contact throughout and finishing with the heel of the palm contacting and controlling the inside of the left Dummy arm. At the same time as the left arm rotates to Kau Sau, the right arm maintains contact, rolling the forearm inwards to form Jum Sau, and pressing forwards and upwards along the right Dummy arm and towards the centre of the Dummy (*see* Fig 125).

46. 45-Degree Juen Ma; Right Kao Sau, Left Jum Sau

Whilst turning to 45 degrees to the other side, circle the left arm clockwise under

CLOCKWISE FROM TOP LEFT:
Fig 152   On guard facing opponent.
Fig 153   Opponent punches; counter Juen Ma, Jum Sau/Wu Sau.
Fig 154   Opponent punches again; counter Juen Ma, Kau Sau/Wan Jeung.
Fig 155   Biu Ma, Gum Sau/Jic Jeung to jaw.

and around the Dummy's arm, maintaining contact throughout, and pulling the elbow and forearm inwards under the Dummy's arm whilst pressing forwards to form Jum Sau. Simultaneously, the right arm maintains contact with the Dummy's arm, circling counter-clockwise around the Dummy's arm to form Kau Sau, and finishing with the heel of the palm contacting and controlling the inside of the Dummy's arm (*see* Fig 126).

In application, Kau Sau can be used with a Juen Ma turning stance, or evasive footwork, either to redirect an opponent's force upon contact or to monitor and control their arm through contact (*see* Fig 154), and is always applied with an instantaneous counter-strike.

In the example below, Kau Sau is used in conjunction with Juen Ma and low side palm strike (Wan Jeung) to the lowest vertebral rib or floating rib. (The first seven ribs attach to the sternum at the front and are known as true or sternal ribs; the lower five ribs do not connect directly to the sternum and are known as false ribs. The upper three of these connect to the costal cartilages of the ribs just above them. The last two false ribs, however, usually have no ventral attachment (no anchor in front) and are referred to as floating or vertebral ribs.). The Kau Sau immediately drops into the centreline and drives up the centreline as a vertical palm strike (Jic Jeung) to the jaw, forcing the head sharply back, whilst the low side palm drops over the opponent's arm and on to their elbow, applying a short, sharp Gum Sau pressing diagonally downward and inwards into their elbow (*see* Fig 155).

47. Face Dummy with Left Jut Sau, Right Jic Jeung

Whilst turning to face the Dummy in a neutral stance, the left Jum Sau switches to Jut Sau, the elbow sharply dragging the wrist in and downwards. At the same time, the Kau Sau elbow quickly drops into the centreline by rolling the right elbow in and down, between the Dummy's arms. The arm is immediately driven up the centreline as a vertical palm strike (Jic Jeung) (*see* Fig 127). As discussed previously, the elbow is slightly off the centreline as it travels forward to the Dummy and can be used to contact and 'control' the Dummy's right arm prior to the palm strike landing. The palm strike should remain relaxed until the fingertips touch the Dummy, and then the palm should be snapped forwards at the wrist (Fa Ging), driven inwards upon contact into the centre of the Dummy and relaxed immediately afterwards. This results in a driven energy from contact, rather than a hit, applying energy into, not on to, the Dummy. As the Dummy rocks on its frame due to the energy of the palm strike, the fingertips should remain in contact with the Dummy's body, monitoring its movement.

The vertical palm strike is ideal for driving into and slightly under the jaw, driving the opponent's head back, which affects the body posture, disrupts the body balance and is extremely painful and temporarily disorienting (*see* Fig 155).

48. 45-Degree Juen Ma; Right Bong Sau, Left Wu Sau

The movement from Jic Jeung to form the Bong Sau has no direct application. However, the arm should be drawn back, the elbow lifted, the forearm rotated, and then the Bong Sau forwarded in order to form the correct structure and position. A common mistake is to simply pivot at the elbow and swing the forearm into the Bong Sau shape.

If the distance from the Dummy has been maintained throughout the previous movements, the Bong Sau should be structured and positioned correctly (*see* previous definition). The relaxed wrist of the Bong Sau arm should make contact at a point within 2in (50mm) of the end of the Dummy's arm, which in this instance represents the outside of an opponent's left wrist (*see* Fig 128). The Wu Sau should be positioned half-way between the wrist and the chin, with the Wu Sau palm covering the throat.

49. 45-Degree Biu Ma, Juen Ma; Right Tan Sau, Left Wan Jeung with Right Jic Gerk

Step (Biu Ma) at approximately 45 degrees to the Dummy, whilst rolling Bong Sau to Tan Sau and maintaining both contact with the Dummy's arm and forward pressure into the Dummy throughout the movement. Whilst stepping, sharply turn the hips and shoulders parallel to the Dummy's leg, transferring the weight on to the left leg whilst simultaneously driving a front kick (Jic Gerk) diagonally upwards and away from the heel of the supporting leg to the side of the knee of the Dummy's leg at approximately 90 degrees to the leg. The left arm can either form a Wu Sau or a Wan Jeung (side palm) to the Dummy's body (*see* Fig

CLOCKWISE FROM TOP LEFT:
Fig 156   On guard facing opponent.
Fig 157   Opponent launches a front kick; counter with a side step and cover.
Fig 158   As the kick lands drive Jic Gerk to the side of the opponent's knee.
Fig 159   Biu Ma, Wan Jeung/Gum Sau.
Fig 160   Juen Ma, Gwoy Jarn/Gum Sau.

129). It is vital to maintain a vertical posture with the hips rolled forwards and to resist the temptation to lean forward to ensure that the side palm makes contact with the Dummy's body.

Applying a front kick at a right angle to the opponent's leg/knee can be used to great effect when defending and countering an opponent's front kick. Stepping to the side to avoid the kick (the best block in the world is to move; *see* Fig 157) ensures that the opponent's kick misses and that the momentum

they used to drive the kick forces the majority of their weight on to their lead leg as the kick lands, putting a lot of stress on to that knee joint.

The knee, one of the most complex and largest joints in the body, is a tough synovial joint that acts like a hinge between the thighbone (the femur) and the shinbone (tibia). As well as bending and straightening, the knee joint also allows rotation and pivoting; however, it does not allow for much lateral movement.

77

As the opponent's lead leg lands, a short, sharp kick to the side of the knee (*see* Fig 158) can cause severe pain, tear the medial collateral ligament and/or the anterior cruciate ligament, and may dislocate the knee entirely. The opponent quite likely will be floored and incapacitated with little or no chance of getting up again quickly. However, should the kick not have the required and desired effect, it is possible to quickly follow up with Biu Ma to close the distance and trap the leg, whilst striking with a side palm to the jaw (*see* Fig 159) and then a Gwoy Jarn elbow strike to the face (*see* Fig 160).

50. Seung Gang Sau

The next movement is to step into a neutral stance (weight 50:50 distribution) with the body at approximately a 45-degree angle to the Dummy and applying Seung Gang Sau into the Dummy (*see* Fig 130). The high Gang Sau arm drives forward to make contact with the Dummy's arm with the inner/upper part of the forearm, the elbow pulled in close to the practitioner's centreline. Simultaneously, the lower Gang Sau forwards and connects with the lower, centre arm of the Dummy with the heel of the right palm. As discussed earlier, the low Gang Sau is similar structurally to Dai Bong Sau in Chum Kiu.

51. Face Dummy, Left Kao Sau, Right Jum Sau

From the Seung Gang Sau position, step in front of and face the Dummy in a neutral stance, whilst maintaining contact and circling the left upper Gang Sau clockwise to form Kau Sau. The combination of the stepping movement and the hip turn create a short, sharp retraction movement on the Dummy as the Kau Sau forms. At the same time, the low Gang Sau cuts upwards as Jum Sau, making contact with the inner/upper part of the forearm about half-way along the ulna and the flexor carpi ulnaris muscle, on to the outside of the Dummy's arm, pressing forwards and upwards from the elbow towards the centre of the Dummy (*see* Fig 131).

In application, as the Kau Sau is applied, the low Gang Sau would probably cut up the centreline and strike the opponent as a punch or palm strike. However, in the Dummy form it is 'intercepted' by the Dummy's arm and therefore converts into Jum Sau.

52. Right Gum Sau, Left Mid Wan Jeung

As soon as the right Jum Sau makes contact with the Dummy's arm, it switches to Gum Sau, whilst turning to face the Dummy in a neutral stance (weight 50:50 distribution); the Kau Sau quickly drops down and into the centreline and drives horizontally along the centreline to strike with Wan Jeung. The side palm strike is the weapon of choice in this instance because its structure is more suitable to mid-level or low-level palm strikes. As discussed previously, the palm strike should remain relaxed until the fingertips touch the Dummy, and then the palm should be snapped forwards (at the same time as Jut Sau is applied), driven inwards upon contact and immediately relaxed afterwards, applying energy into, not on to, the Dummy. As the Dummy rocks on its frame due to the energy of the palm strike, the fingertips should remain in contact with the Dummy's body, monitoring its movement (*see* Fig 132).

In application, the Gum Sau energy sharply pulls down the opponent's arm, therefore a high palm strike is more likely to be applied (*see* Fig 164).

53. 45-Degree Juen Ma, Left Bong Sau, Right Wu Sau

The movement from Wan Jeung to form the Bong Sau is largely irrelevant, as it has no direct application. However, the arm should

CLOCKWISE FROM TOP LEFT:
Fig 161   On guard facing opponent.
Fig 162   Opponent punches; Juen Ma, Seung Gang Sau.
Fig 163   Opponent throws second punch; Juen Ma, convert low Gang Sau to Jum Sau.
Fig 164   Juen Ma, Gum Sau/Wan Jeung.
Fig 165   Follow with Juen Ma, Jic Kuen to face.

be drawn back slightly, the elbow lifted over the Dummy's arm, the forearm rotated, and then the Bong Sau forwarded into position. A common mistake is to simply pivot at the elbow and swing the forearm into the Bong Sau shape.

Furthermore, as discussed earlier, if the distance from the Dummy has been maintained throughout the previous movements, then the Bong Sau structure should be correct (*see* previous definition). The relaxed wrist of the Bong Sau arm should make contact at a point within 2in (50mm) of the end of the Dummy's arm, which in this instance represents the outside of an opponent's left wrist (*see* Fig 133).

54. 45-Degree Biu Ma, Juen Ma; Left Tan Sau, Right Wan Jeung with Left Jic Gerk

Step (Biu Ma) at approximately 45 degrees whilst rolling Bong Sau to Tan Sau and maintaining contact with the Dummy's arm and forward pressure into the Dummy.

79

Fig 166   On guard facing opponent.

Fig 167   Opponent launches right punch; counter Juen Ma, Bong Sau/Wu Sau.

Immediately turn, transferring the weight on to the right leg and turning the hips and body perpendicular to the Dummy's leg. As soon as the body and hips turn, drive a front kick (Jic Gerk) to the side of the knee of the Dummy's leg. The right arm can form either a Wu Sau or Wan Jeung (side palm) to the Dummy's body (*see* Fig 134). Again, it is vital

Fig 168 Opponent throws second punch; counter Juen Ma, Tan Sau/Wan Jeung, Jic Gerk to side of the knee.

Fig 169 Follow step in, Gwoy Jarn/Gum Sau.

to maintain a vertical posture, with the hips rolled forwards, and resist the temptation to lean forward to ensure that the side palm makes contact.

When applying Jic Gerk, it is essential not to 'chamber' the kick – retract the foot in order to try to develop more power. The foot should always be ahead of the knee, so that it can be used effectively and efficiently from the moment it leaves the ground. Should the foot be chambered in a vain attempt to increase the power of the kick, it is possible for an opponent at close proximity to quickly step in and jam the kick, trapping the chambered leg and foot as it retracts, leaving the Wing Chun practitioner trapped, vulnerable and off balance. The leg should be lifted at the knee, and the foot thrust diagonally upward and forward, though not to full extension, to intercept an opponent's kick, cover the centreline or, in this instance, to strike the side of the knee joint (*see* Fig 168).

55. Seung Gang Sau

The next movement is to step into a neutral stance (weight 50:50 distribution) at approximately a 45-degree angle to the Dummy with Seung Gang Sau as discussed previously (*see* Fig 135).

56. Face Dummy with Right Kao Sau, Left Jum Sau

From the Gang Sau step to face the Dummy in a neutral stance, maintaining contact with the high right Gang Sau and circling counterclockwise to form Kau Sau, as detailed previously. The step and the hip turn together create a short, sharp retraction as the Kau Sau forms. At the same time, the low Gang Sau cuts upwards and up the centreline towards the 'head' of the Dummy. Since the Dummy's arms are fixed in position, the left arm is 'intercepted' by the Dummy's arm and therefore converts into Jum Sau on to the outside of the Dummy's arm, contacting with the inner/upper part of the forearm (*see* Fig 136).

57. Face Dummy with Left Jut Sau, Right Jic Jeung

As soon as the left Jum Sau makes contact with the Dummy's arm, it converts to Jut Sau. At the same time, the Kau Sau elbow rolls into the centreline and then drives up

the centreline to strike above the Dummy's arms with Jic Jeung, remaining relaxed until fingertip contact (*see* Fig 137).

Section 5

This section introduces Po Pai Jeung.

Po Pai Jeung

Po Pai – Cantonese term meaning **pushing palms**.
Jeung – Cantonese term meaning **palm** *n.*, inner part of hand from wrist to base of the fingers.

Po Pai Jeung is a double pushing palm application, using a vertical palm and an inverted palm. It is applied by driving both arms forward along the centreline with the hands and fingers relaxed. As soon as the fingers make contact with the body, press forward and slightly downwards with both palms. As soon as firm resistance is felt, apply a short, sharp push into the body from the elbows, snapping the wrists forward and slightly upwards, and then immediately relaxing the hands and the fingers. This results in a driven energy from contact, rather than a hit, applying energy into, not on to, the Dummy.

Checklist

- Make initial contact with the fingertips.
- Upon contact drive the palms forward and downwards from the elbows.
- Use the body mass to give power to the Po Pai Jeung.
- Immediately relax the hands once Po Pai Jeung has been applied.

Section 5: Moves 58–72

58. Right Biu Jut Sau to left Dummy arm.
59. Right Biu Jut Sau to right Dummy arm.

Figs 170 and 171   Po Pai Jeung makes initial light contact, and then applies a short, sharp energy.

60. Right Jum Sau to left Dummy arm.
61. Turn right Kao Sau, plus left low Wan Jeung.
62. Kwun Sau.
63. Face with Po Pai Jeung.

64. Turn left Bong Sau, right Wu Sau.
65. 45-Degree step in with Po Pai Jeung.
66. Seung Gang Sau at approximately 45 degrees to Dummy.
67. Face Dummy with Po Pai Jeung.

Fig 172   Right Biu Jut Sau.   Fig 173   Right Biu Jut Sau.   Fig 174   Right Jum Sau.

Fig 175   Turn right Kao Sau, plus left low Wan Jeung.

Fig 176   Kwun Sau.

Fig 177   Face with Po Pai Jeung.

Fig 178   Turn left Bong Sau, right Wu Sau.

Fig 179   45-Degree step in with Po Pai Jeung.

Fig 180   Seung Gang Sau at approximately 45 degrees to Dummy.

68. Turn right Bong Sau, left Wu Sau.
69. Step in 45 degrees, Po Pai Jeung.
70. Seung Gang Sau at approximately 45 degrees to Dummy.
71. Face, left Kao Sau, right Jum Sau.
72. Right Jut Sau, left low Wan Jeung.

Fig 181 Face Dummy with Po Pai Jeung.

Fig 182 Turn right Bong Sau, left Wu Sau.

Fig 183 Step in 45 degrees, Po Pai Jeung.

Fig 184 Seung Gang Sau at approximately 45 degrees to Dummy.

Fig 185 Face, left Kao Sau, right Jum Sau.

Fig 186 Right Jut Sau, left low Wan Jeung.

58. Right Biu Jut Sau (Fut Sau)

From the right Jic Jeung (*see* Fig 137) drop the elbow into the centreline, at the same time bringing the left hand into the centreline as Wu Sau. Flick the right wrist across to the left Dummy arm as Biu Jut Sau, effectively pivoting at the right elbow, contacting on the inside of the right wrist with a slight Jut Sau

85

CLOCKWISE FROM TOP LEFT:
Fig 187   On guard facing opponent.
Fig 188   Opponent punches; counter Juen Ma, Biu Jut Sau/Wu Sau.
Fig 189   Instantly drive Jic Kuen up the centreline with Tan Sau cover.
Fig 190   Counter the opponent's second punch with Juen Ma, Tan Da.

retracting energy (*see* Fig 172). It is important not to impact the Dummy's arm with the radius bone (on the outside edge of the forearm). The contact should be more on the underside of the forearm, along the brachioradialis muscle.

In application, the Biu Jut Sau can be used to quickly cover and control a strike (*see* Fig 188), and then, using the Wing Chun concept of Lut Sau Jic Chung (hand lost, spring forward), instantly drive forward, up and along the centreline as the opponent's punch begins to retract, covering with Tan Sau (*see* Fig 189). Should the opponent attempt a second strike, simply turn with Tan Sau, Wan Jeung to the face (*see* Fig 190).

59. Right Biu Jut Sau (Fut Sau)

Flick the right wrist across to the right Dummy arm, contacting on the outside of the right wrist with a slight Jut Sau retracting energy, whilst the left arm/hand remains in Wu Sau (*see* Fig 173).

CLOCKWISE FROM TOP LEFT:
Fig 191   On guard facing opponent.
Fig 192   Opponent punches; counter Juen Ma, Biu Jut Sau/Wu Sau.
Fig 193   Opponent punches again; counter Juen Ma right Biu Jut Sau/Wu Sau.
Fig 194   Opponent throws another punch; Juen Ma, Jum Sau/Wu Sau.
Fig 195   Follow with Juen Ma, Kau Sau/Chao Kuen to floating rib.
(Sequence continued on page 88.)

60. 45-Degree Juen Ma, Right Jum Sau, Left Wu Sau

Roll the right Jum Sau across to the left Dummy arm, effectively rolling the right elbow clockwise into the centreline, in conjunction with a turning stance (Juen Ma) contacting on the outside of the right wrist. At the same time, the left arm/hand remains in Wu Sau (*see* Fig 174).

The Fut Sau/Jum Sau combination can be used in application under certain circumstances; for example, against a quick succession of jabs (*see* Figs 192–194) Jum Sau can naturally flow into Kau Sau as punches tend to curve inwards towards the centre due to the natural hip/spinal rotation of the opponent's punching action (*see* Fig 195).

61. 45-Degree Juen Ma, Right Kao Sau, Left Wan Jeung

Turn to 45 degrees, circle the right arm over and around the Dummy's arm counter-clockwise from Jum Sau, maintaining contact throughout with the wrist and lifting

(Cont. from page 87)
CLOCKWISE FROM TOP LEFT:
Fig 196   Follow with double Lap Sau and knee strike.
Fig 197   Follow with Jic Gerk to knee.

the elbow to form Kau Sau. Simultaneously, the left arm drives forward horizontally as a mid-level palm strike (Wan Jeung), contacting and striking with the base of the palm, effectively the end of the ulna and radius bones (*see* Fig 175).

62. Kwun Sau

Kwun Sau is a combination of Tan Sau and Dai Bong Sau to create a < shape, giving a greater field of cover. As the Wan Jeung is withdrawn, the wrist is lowered and the elbow raised and rolled forward clockwise to form Dai Bong Sau, as per Chum Kiu. At the same time, the Kau Sau is drawn in, the elbow pulled into the centreline, and the forearm rotated clockwise, to form Tan Sau. Both arms are then driven forwards together to make contact with the Dummy's arms. Dai Bong Sau uses the flat face of the forearm (extensor carpi ulnaris, extensor digiti minimi and extensor digitorum muscles), which presses forward and in towards the Dummy upon contact with the low, middle Dummy's arm, whilst Tan Sau contacts the upper Dummy's arm using the outside lower edge of the forearm (extensor digitorum muscle) (*see* Fig 176).

63. Face with Po Pai Jeung

Turn to face the Dummy, converting the Kwun Sau (Tan Sau and Dai Bong Sau) into Po Pai Jeung. From the Tan Sau position, draw the wrist into the centreline, rotating the forearm anticlockwise, to form Jic Jeung, whilst turning to face the Dummy in a neutral stance. Simultaneously, roll the left elbow into the centreline, rotating the forearm anticlockwise and pushing the left wrist forward in a reverse Jic Jeung structure, and then drive both arms forward along the centreline with the hands and fingers relaxed. As soon as both palms make light contact with the Dummy's body, apply a short, sharp push into the Dummy from the elbows, snapping the wrists forward (*see* Fig 177) and then immediately relaxing the hands and the fingers. This results in a driven energy from contact, rather than a hit, applying energy into, not on to, the Dummy. As the Dummy rocks on its frame or base due to the energy of the palm strike, the fingertips should remain in contact with the Dummy's body, monitoring its movement.

In photographs, it is difficult to show the application of energy, so the photographs

CLOCKWISE FROM TOP LEFT:
Fig 198   Chi Sau – partner A on the left, B on the right.
Fig 199   Partner A rolls to Bong Sau.
Fig 200   Partner A turns to form Bong Sau/Wu.
Fig 201   Partner A applies Lap Sau and commences a Fak Sau strike.
Fig 202   Partner B counters the Bong Sau, Lap Sau with Juen Ma, Kwun Sau.
(Sequence continued on page 90.)

used show the arm positions as the forward energy is being applied.

In fighting application, Po Pai Jeung is rarely used because it utilizes and therefore commits both hands. However, in Chi Sau it is an excellent tool to control an opponent, use their force and balance (or lack of it) against them and then 'dispose' of them. Using Po Pai Jeung within Chi Sau is similar to using a full stop at the end of a sentence; it signifies and provides an indisputable end to the sequence. This is not to suggest that Po Pai Jeung cannot be used in a fighting application under certain circumstances, or that it cannot be applied successfully in a combat scenario. I have therefore chosen to show some applications of Po Pai Jeung in both a Chi Sau and combat context.

64. 45-Degree Juen Ma Left Bong Sau, Right Wu Sau

The movement from the lower Po Pai Jeung to form the Bong Sau is for the most part extraneous because it has no specific application.

(Cont. from page 89)
CLOCKWISE FROM TOP LEFT:
Fig 203   Partner B quickly converts Kwun Sau to Po Pai Jeung.
Fig 204   Partner B applies Po Pai energy.

However, in order to form the Bong Sau correctly, the arm should be drawn back slightly, the elbow lifted over the left Dummy arm, the forearm rotated clockwise, and the Bong Sau forwarded into position on the inside gate of the right Dummy arm. If the optimal distance from the Dummy has been maintained throughout the previous sequence of movements, then the Bong Sau should be correct in both structure and position (*see* previous definition). The relaxed wrist of the Bong Sau arm should make contact at a point within 2in (50mm) of the end of the Dummy's arm, which in this case represents the inside of an opponent's arm.

The upper Po Pai Jeung is retracted slightly at the elbow, the elbow dropped, and the arm repositioned as Wu Sau and driven forward along the Wing Chun practitioner's centreline at the same time as the Bong Sau travels forward (*see* Fig 178).

65. 45-Degree Step In with Po Pai Jeung
The Bong Sau to Po Pai Jeung, in conjunction with stepping around the Dummy's leg and repositioning at approximately 45 degrees, is one of the core techniques of the fifth section of the Dummy. It is essential

that the timing and coordination are correct, so that the Po Pai Jeung and foot contact arrive powerfully and simultaneously. Whilst stepping, re-angling and moving around the Dummy, the Bong Sau must maintain both contact with the Dummy's arm and forward pressure along it and towards the body of the Dummy as it rotates anticlockwise to form the upper Po Pai Jeung structure (similar to Jic Jeung). At the same time as the Bong Sau rotates, the Wu Sau drops at the wrist into the Wing Chun practitioner's centreline and the forearm rotates clockwise to form the lower Po Pai Jeung. If the footwork is correct, the practitioner will be in the best possible position to apply the hand and leg techniques powerfully (*see* Fig 179). Po Pai Jeung is again applied as described previously.

66. Seung Gang Sau
Step into a neutral stance (50:50 weight distribution) at approximately a 45-degree angle to the Dummy with Seung Gang Sau (*see* Fig 180). The high Gang Sau arm drives forward to make contact with the Dummy's arm with the inner/upper part of the forearm, about half-way along the ulna and flexor carpi ulnaris muscle, with the elbow pulled

CLOCKWISE FROM TOP LEFT:
Fig 205   On guard facing opponent.
Fig 206   Opponent punches; counter Juen Ma, Bong Chor Sau/Wu Sau.
Fig 207   Opponent retracts punch ready for second punch; counter stick and follow in with Po Pai Jeung.
Fig 208   Apply Po Pai energy.

in close to the practitioner's centreline. Simultaneously, the low Gang Sau forwards and connects with the lower, centre arm of the Dummy with the heel of the right palm. The low Gang Sau is similar in shape and structure to the Dai Bong Sau practised in Chum Kiu. If the body position is correct when stepping with the double Gang Sau, then both arms will be in contact with the Dummy's arms with the correct vertical body posture, shoulders relaxed and a strong neutral stance.

67. Face Dummy with Po Pai Jeung

Step into a neutral stance in front of the Dummy, whilst applying Po Pai Jeung. The high Gang Sau forearm rotates anticlockwise into the centreline to form the upper Po Pai Jeung, whilst the lower Gang Sau wrist is rotated anticlockwise as it is driven forward and into the centreline to form the lower Po Pai Jeung. Both arms are then driven forward, with the hands and wrists relaxed towards the Dummy to apply Po Pai Jeung as discussed earlier (*see* Fig 181).

CLOCKWISE FROM TOP LEFT:
Fig 209   Chi Sau – partner A on the left, B on the right.
Fig 210   Partner A rolls to Bong Sau.
Fig 211   Partner A turns to form Bong Sau/Wu.
Fig 212   Partner A applies Lap Sau and commences a low punch towards the ribs.
Fig 213   Partner B counters with Juen Ma, Seung Gang Sau.
(Sequence continued opposite.)

68. 45-Degree Juen Ma Right Bong Sau, Left Wu Sau

The movement from the upper Po Pai Jeung to form the Bong Sau is, for the most part, superfluous and has no specific application. However, in order to form the Bong Sau correctly, the arm should be drawn back slightly, the elbow lifted over the right Dummy arm, the forearm rotated anticlockwise, and then the Bong Sau forwarded into position on the inside gate of the left Dummy arm, which in this instance can represent the outside of

an opponent's arm. The Bong Sau structure should be correct (*see* previous definition) if the optimal distance from the Dummy has been maintained throughout the previous sequence of movements. The relaxed wrist of the Bong Sau arm should make contact at a point within 2in (50mm) of the end of the Dummy's arm.

The lower Po Pai Jeung is slightly retracted at the elbow, the wrist lifted, and the arm repositioned as Wu Sau and driven forward along the Wing Chun practitioner's centreline

Left: Fig 214   Partner B
converts Seung Gang Sau
to Po Pai Jeung.
Right: Fig 215   Apply Po
Pai energy.

at the same time as the Bong Sau travels forward (*see* Fig 182).

69. 45-Degree Step In with Po Pai Jeung

The difference between this technique and the Po Pai Jeung on the other side of the Dummy (movement 65) is that whilst stepping, re-angling and moving around the Dummy, the Bong Sau disengages from the Dummy's arm to form the lower Po Pai Jeung structure.

The disengaging and rapid re-engaging contact with the Dummy is the key to this technique; it should be done with the minimal amount of movement and without actually withdrawing the hands and then impacting hard to regain contact. As the Bong Sau drops and rotates to form the lower Po Pai Jeung, the Wu Sau drives forward to form the upper Po Pai Jeung (Jic Jeung).

As soon as the Po Pai Jeung makes light contact with the Dummy's body, a short, sharp push into the Dummy from the elbows is applied, snapping the wrists forward and then immediately relaxing the hands and the fingers (*see* Fig 183).

As stated previously, if the footwork is correct, the practitioner will be in the best possible position to apply the hand and leg techniques powerfully. This sequence or technique can be applied, for example, against an attacker's one–two punch combination.

The Bong Sau to Po Pai Jeung, in conjunction with stepping around the Dummy's leg and repositioning at 45 degrees, is one of the core techniques of the fifth section of the Dummy. It is essential that the timing and coordination are correct, so that the Po Pai Jeung and foot contact arrive powerfully and simultaneously.

70. Seung Gang Sau

This is a mirrored repeat of movement 66 (*see* Fig 184).

71. Face with Left Kao Sau, Right Jum Sau

From the Seung Gang Sau position, step in front of and face the Dummy in a neutral stance, whilst maintaining contact and circling the left upper Gang Sau clockwise to form Kau Sau. The combination of the stepping movement and the hip turn create a short, sharp retraction movement on the Dummy's arm as the Kau Sau forms. At the same time, the low Gang Sau

CLOCKWISE FROM TOP LEFT:
Fig 216   On guard facing opponent.
Fig 217   Opponent punches; counter Juen Ma, Bong Sau/Wu Sau.
Fig 218   Opponent throws second punch; counter Juen Ma, position for Po Pai Jeung.
Fig 219   Biu Ma in, Po Pai Jeung, controlling opponent's foot.
Fig 220   Apply Po Pai Jeung energy.

cuts upwards as Jum Sau, making contact with the inner/upper part of the forearm on to the outside of the right Dummy arm, pressing forwards and upwards from the elbow towards the centre of the Dummy (*see* Fig 185).

In application, as the Kau Sau is applied to the outside gate of an opponent's punch, the low Gang Sau would probably cut up and along the centreline and strike the opponent as a punch or palm strike. However, on the Dummy it is 'intercepted'

by the Dummy's arm and therefore converts into Jum Sau.

72. Face Dummy with Right Jut Sau, Left Wan Jeung

As soon as the right Jum Sau makes contact with the Dummy's arm, it converts to Jut Sau. At the same time, the Kau Sau elbow rolls into the centreline and drives along the centreline to strike below the Dummy's arms with Wan Jeung, remaining relaxed until fingertip contact (*see* Fig 186).

Section 6: Moves 73–87

73. 45-Degree left Juen Ma, Seung Gang Sau.
74. 45-Degree right Juen Ma, Seung Gang Sau.
75. 45-Degree left Juen Ma, right Bong Sau, left Wu Sau.
76. 45-Degree right Juen Ma, Lap Sau, left Fak Da.
77. Face with left Gum Sau, right Wan Jeung.
78. 45-Degree right Juen Ma, left Bong Sau, right Wu Sau.
79. 45-Degree left Juen Ma, left Lap Sau, right Fak Da.
80. Face, right Gum Sau, left Wan Jeung.
81. 45-Degree left Juen Ma, right Bong Sau, left Wu Sau.
82. Step 45 degrees, right Tan Sau, left mid Wan Jeung and left Chut Sun Jic Gerk.
83. Step back, left Bong Sau, right Wu Sau.
84. Step 45 degrees with left Tan Sau, right low Wan Jeung and right Chut Sun Jic Gerk.
85. Step back, Seung Gang Sau at approximately 45 degrees to Dummy in a neutral stance.
86. Face, right Kao Sau, left Jum Sau.
87. Left Jut Sau, right Jic Jeung.

73. 45-Degree Left Juen Ma, Seung Gang Sau

Double Gang Sau, sometimes referred to as high and low Gang Sau, is a complex, two-handed defensive structure designed to give maximum body cover in order to gain useful and informative contact with an opponent's attack. At first, it can appear to be simply a combination of Tan Sau and Dai Bong Sau. However, the structures and the energies employed in this combination are quite different and unique. The upper Gang Sau is visually and structurally similar to Tan Sau, although it is actually more akin to Jum Sau in its energy and its use. The upper Gang Sau uses the inside edge of the forearm, about half-way along

Fig 221   45-Degree left Juen Ma, Seung Gang Sau.

Fig 222   45-Degree right Juen Ma, Seung Gang Sau.

Fig 223   45-Degree left Juen Ma, right Bong Sau, left Wu Sau.

Fig 224   45-Degree right Juen Ma, Lap Sau, left Fak Da.

Fig 225   Face with left Gum Sau, right Wan Jeung.

Fig 226   45-Degree right Juen Ma, left Bong Sau, right Wu Sau.

Fig 227   45-Degree left Juen Ma, left Lap Sau, right Fak Da.

Fig 228   Face, right Gum Sau, left Wan Jeung.

Fig 229   45-Degree left Juen Ma, right Bong Sau, left Wu Sau.

the ulna and flexor carpi ulnaris muscles and ulna bone, with the elbow pulled in and tucked down close to the centreline. The elbow and forearm are driven up and along the centreline, stopping at the fixed elbow position.

Used in conjunction with a shallow turning stance, the upper Gang Sau gains

Fig 230 Step 45 degrees, right Tan Sau, left Wan Jeung and left Chut Sun Jic Gerk.

Fig 231 Step back, left Bong Sau, right Wu Sau.

Fig 232 Step 45 degrees with left Tan Sau, right Wan Jeung and right Chut Sun Jic Gerk.

Fig 233 Step back, Seung Gang Sau at approximately 45 degrees to Dummy in a neutral stance.

Fig 234 Face, right Kao Sau, left Jum Sau.

Fig 235 Left Jut Sau, right Jic Jeung.

and maintains contact with an opponent's arm, keeping both the wrist and the elbow close to the centreline. The wrist stays higher than the elbow to cover and protect the upper half of the torso, whilst the fingers aim towards the opponent's face or throat area as a deterrent from stepping or moving closer.

The lower Gang Sau is visually and structurally similar to Dai Bong Sau (low Bong Sau). It uses the same leading edge of the forearm as the upper Gang Sau to receive an opponent's mid-level strike and protect the lower half of the torso. As the body angles, the lower Gang Sau drives forward, keeping the wrist on the centreline; the elbow stops at the fixed elbow position at about sternum height.

In order to provide successful body cover of the torso, the wrists of the upper and lower Gang Sau should both be on the centreline (i.e. one above the other) and both elbows should be about the same height, slightly overlapping to create a > shape coverage (*see* Fig 221).

74. 45-Degree Right Juen Ma, Seung Gang Sau

The mechanics of turning from one side to the other correctly are quite complex to perform and even more difficult to explain accurately in writing. As the body begins to turn in order to angle to the other side, both the lower and upper Gang Sau rotate around the centre of the forearm. The lower Gang Sau rotates anticlockwise, drawing the elbow in and down toward the centreline, finishing in the upper Gang Sau structure.

At the same time, the upper Gang Sau rotates anticlockwise, pulling the wrist downwards, although still on the centreline, and ending in the upper Gang Sau structure. As soon as the arms have rotated and swapped shapes, the body is angled sharply to the other side, driving both of the Gang Sau forward via the elbow along the centreline to the fixed elbow distance (*see* Fig 222).

75. 45-Degree Left Juen Ma, Right Bong Sau, Left Wu Sau

The movement from Seung Gang Sau to form the Bong Sau is largely irrelevant in that it has no direct application. However, the path taken to form Bong Sau should be precise in order to initiate a good structure and practise the correct formation of the Bong Sau. The lower Gang Sau arm should be lifted at the elbow, bringing the wrist into the Wing Chun practitioner's centreline over the right Dummy arm, and the Bong Sau (in this instance representing Bong Chor Sau) and the supporting Wu Sau forwarded to make contact on the left Dummy arm, the end of the Dummy's arm representing an opponent's wrist (*see* Fig 223).

76. 45-Degree Right Juen Ma, Right Lap Sau, Left Fak Da

The transition from Bong Chor Sau to form the Lap Sau can feel an awkward movement and the resulting Lap Sau arm position does not necessarily feel comfortable. This is because, in application, the Lap Sau would pull, deflect and reposition the attacker's arm; on the Dummy, however, the arm cannot move and so the Lap Sau can feel a little cramped if incorrectly positioned. The key is to develop a smooth and powerful transition from Bong Chor Sau, through to the Lap Sau position, apply the necessary Lap Sau energy and simultaneously deliver a powerful Fak Sau strike (not actually striking the Dummy's body hard).

The Bong Chor Sau to Lap Sau/Fak Sau movement, in conjunction with turning (Juen Ma) at 45 degrees on the outside gate (*see* Fig 224), is one of the core techniques of this section of the Dummy. It is essential that the timing and coordination are correct, so that the Lap Sau and Fak Sau are carried out powerfully and simultaneously.

Whilst re-angling to the outside gate of the Dummy, the Bong Sau must maintain both contact with the Dummy's arm and forward pressure along it towards the body of the Dummy. The elbow drops in towards the centreline, pivoting around the Dummy's arm and maintaining contact as it rotates

Fig 236   On guard facing opponent.

Fig 237   Opponent punches; counter Juen Ma, Seung Gang Sau.

Fig 238   Opponent throws second punch; counter Seung Gang Sau.

Fig 239   Step in Gwoy Jarn, Gum Sau.

Fig 240   Follow with Man Geng Sau, knee strike.

Fig 241   Follow in Jic Gerk to opponent's knee.

and then converts to Lap Sau upon completion of the turning stance. At the same time as the Lap Sau is carried out, the Wu Sau elbow lifts until the forearm is parallel to the floor; the elbow drives the relaxed wrist forward along the centreline towards the Dummy. When the relaxed Fak Sau hand makes contact with the Dummy, the wrist snaps the energy into the Dummy, then immediately relaxes again.

77. Face Dummy with Left Gum Sau, Right Wan Jeung

Turn to face the Dummy in a neutral stance with a left Gum Sau and a right side palm strike (Wan Jeung) (*see* Fig 225). The Fak Sau sharply drops inwards and downwards to drop on to the end of the Dummy's arm as a Gum Sau, the elbow of which is down at an approximate 45-degree angle. At the same time, the Lap Sau drives forward as a high palm strike, remaining relaxed until contact with the Dummy, then snapping the energy into the Dummy using a sharp contraction of the triceps and the wrist.

As discussed earlier, it is debatable whether the left-hand technique should be a Gum Sau or a Jut Sau. It is difficult to say that it should be one, rather than the other, as they can both be applied on the Dummy and in application. However, in this particular application, Gum Sau is preferable.

In application, the left Gum Sau drops down and inwards heavily on to the opponent's elbow, using the power from the hips as the practitioner turns to face the opponent to maximize the power of the Gum Sau. This diagonal downward and inward energy disrupts the opponent's balance and posture and severely limits his or her ability to launch an efficient second strike due to poor and inefficient posture and positioning. At the same time as the Gum Sau is applied, the Wing Chun practitioner strikes to the head, usually the face and in particular the mandible (jaw) (*see* Fig 247).

In application, the Bong Sau can be applied either to the inside or outside gate of a punch. If applied to the outside gate, as shown in the example below (*see* Fig 243), the Lap Sau can be used to intercept a second punch and used simultaneously with a Fak Sau counter strike (*see* Fig 245). The Gum Sau/Wan Jeung can be used as an immediate follow up, the Wan Jeung driving into the opponent's jaw (*see* Fig 247) to simultaneously strike and act

as a control point, preventing the opponent turning to strike again without risk of injury to their neck.

78. 45-Degree Right Juen Ma, Left Bong Sau, Right Wu Sau

This movement is a mirror of movement 75, except that the Bong Sau is formed from the previous left Gum Sau position (*see* Fig 226). Although actual movement from Gum Sau to form the Bong Sau has no direct application, the path taken to form Bong Sau should be precise in order to initiate a good structure and practise the correct formation of the Bong Sau. The Gum Sau arm should be slightly withdrawn, then the forearm and elbow rotated clockwise, bringing the wrist into the Wing Chun practitioner's centreline, and the Bong Sau and the supporting Wu Sau forwarded to make contact on the Dummy's arm.

79. 45-Degree Left Juen Ma, Left Lap Sau, Right Fak Da

This movement is a mirror of movement 76 (*see* Fig 227).

80. Face, Right Gum Sau, Left Wan Jeung

This movement is a mirror of movement 77 (*see* Fig 228).

81. 45-Degree Left Juen Ma, Right Bong Sau, Left Wu Sau

This movement is the same as movement 75, except that the Bong Sau is formed from the previous right Gum Sau position (*see* Fig 229).

82. Step 45 Degrees, Right Tan Sau, Left Mid Wan Jeung and Left Chut Sun Jic Gerk

From Bong Sau step 45 degrees and turn to face the Dummy – right Tan Sau, left Wan Jeung and left Chut Sun Gerk (*see* Fig

Fig 242   On guard facing partner.

Fig 243   Opponent punches; counter Juen Ma, Bong Sau/Wu Sau.

Fig 244   Quickly follow with Juen Ma, Lap Sau and begin Fak Sau.

Fig 245   Lap Sau, Fak Da to throat.

Fig 246   Juen Ma, half Gum Sau/Wan Jeung.

Fig 247   Gum Sau/Wan Jeung to Jaw.

230). This is one of the core techniques of the sixth section of the Dummy, and it is essential that the timing and coordination are correct so that the Tan Sau, Wan Jeung and the kick arrive powerfully and simultaneously.

In order to perform this kick powerfully and successfully having stepped at 45 degrees with Biu Ma, the Wing Chun practitioner must bring his right foot momentarily next to his left foot, keeping the weight on the right foot, whilst turning the feet and the body to face the centre of the Dummy. Only then can the left cross-stamp kick (Chut Sun Gerk) be driven diagonally upwards and forwards from the supporting leg into the Dummy's body along the Tse M Seen. The kick should land simultaneously with the forming of the Tan Sau and the applying of the side palm strike (Wan Jeung). As soon as the kick has landed, the left foot should be placed back on the ground, next to the right foot. The Tse M Seen can be considered a centreline plane that radiates out from the centre of an opponent (or Dummy) through 360 degrees. When practising on the Dummy, this plane is defined as the line that joins the centreline of the Wing Chun practitioner to the centreline of the Dummy. It is this line (plane) that a Wing Chun exponent practises to dominate and to defend and counter-attack along, both with the upper and the lower limbs. In reality, it can be quite difficult, often impractical, to make contact on the Dummy with the Tan Sau whilst kicking, without distorting the upper body posture. It is therefore equally viable and correct to use a Wu Sau instead of a Tan Sau to ensure the correct body posture and kicking structure (*see* Fig 248).

Whilst stepping, re-angling and moving around the Dummy, the Bong Sau must maintain both contact with the Dummy's arm and forward pressure along it, towards the body of the Dummy. If the footwork is correct, and therefore the practitioner's position is correct relative to the Dummy, they will be in the best possible position to apply the hand and leg techniques powerfully and will have three points of contact on the Dummy (*see* Fig 230):

1. The right Tan Sau wrist on the end of the Dummy's arm.
2. The left side palm strike to the Dummy trunk.
3. The left heel of the kick on the Dummy trunk.

Fig 248   Chut Sun Jic Gerk with the Wu Sau cover.

If the distance is incorrect, the palm strike will not reach; if the angle is incorrect, then either the Tan Sau or the side palm will not make contact correctly; if the distance around the Dummy is not correct, then the kick will not be touching the Dummy's body. Only one position can be correct, which is one of the great benefits of Wooden Dummy training.

In application, the cross-stamp kick can be used at close quarters to destroy the stance, body posture and structure of an opponent. For example, if the Bong Sau is deployed to receive a punch on the outside gate of an opponent's arm (*see* Fig 250) and the opponent immediately retracts and throws a second punch, the Wu Sau can be quickly

CLOCKWISE FROM TOP LEFT:
Fig 249   On guard facing partner.
Fig 250   Opponent punches; counter 45-degree Bong Sau/Wu Sau.
Fig 251   Opponent throws second punch; Biu Ma, trap the leg, Jic Kuen, Pak Sau cover to elbow.
Fig 252   Sharply turn the lead leg into opponent's knee.
Fig 253   Sharp cross-stamp kick to back of opponent's knee.

converted into Pak Sau on the outside gate of the second punch with a simultaneous centreline punch, whilst stepping into the centreline to find contact with the opponent's leg (*see* Fig 251). Upon contact with the opponent's lower leg, a short, sharp outward rotation of the lead leg (*see* Fig 252) causes a slight disruption in the opponent's posture and weight distribution, allowing the Wing Chun practitioner to move in with a cross-stamp kick to the back of the opponent's knee (*see* Fig 253), specifically to the lateral

head of the gastrocnemius. This causes damage to the ligaments, a loss of stance and the opponent falls away from the Wing Chun practitioner.

83. Step Back Left Bong Sau, Right Wu Sau

Take a short Biu Ma step parallel to the Dummy frame whilst forwarding a left Bong Sau on to the right Dummy arm, covering with a right Wu Sau. To correctly form the Bong Sau, the Wan Jeung is slightly retracted and lifted at the elbow, whilst rotated clockwise and rolled forwards over the left Dummy arm to contact almost at the end of the right Dummy arm with the Bong Sau wrist. In unison, the right Tan Sau is slightly withdrawn and rotated beneath the forming Bong Sau, then forwarded to form the supporting Wu Sau (*see* Fig 231).

84. Step 45 Degrees, Left Tan Sau, Right Wan Jeung, Right Chut Sun Jic Gerk
This is a mirror repeat of movement 82 (*see* Fig 232).

85. Seung Gang Sau
Step into a neutral stance (50:50 weight distribution) at approximately a 45-degree angle to the Dummy with Seung Gang Sau (*see* Fig 233). The high Gang Sau arm drives forward to make contact with the Dummy's arm with the inner/upper part of the forearm, about half-way along the ulna and flexor carpi ulnaris muscle, with the elbow pulled in close to the practitioner's centreline. Simultaneously, the lower Gang Sau forwards and connects with the lower, centre arm of the Dummy with the heel of the right palm. The low Gang Sau is similar in shape and structure to the Dai Bong Sau practised in Chum Kiu. If the body position is correct when stepping with the double Gang Sau, both arms will be in contact with the Dummy's arms with the correct vertical body posture, shoulders relaxed and a strong neutral stance.

86. Face with Right Kao Sau, Left Jum Sau
From the Gang Sau, step to face the Dummy in a neutral stance, maintaining contact with the high right Gang Sau and circling counter-clockwise to form Kau Sau, as detailed previously. The step and the hip turn together create a short, sharp retraction as the Kau Sau forms; at the same time the low Gang

Sau cuts upwards and up the centreline towards the 'head' of the Dummy. Since the Dummy's arms are fixed in position, the left arm is 'intercepted' by the Dummy's arm and therefore converts into Jum Sau on to the outside of the Dummy's arm, contacting with the inner/upper part of the forearm (*see* Fig 234).

87. Face Dummy with Left Jut Sau, Right Jic Jeung
As soon as the left Jum Sau makes contact with the Dummy's arm, it converts to Jut Sau. At the same time, the Kau Sau elbow rolls into the centreline and then drives up the centreline to strike above the Dummy's arms with Jic Jeung, remaining relaxed until fingertip contact (*see* Fig 235). As soon as this movement has been completed, the right

Fig 254   By Jong intermediary position.

arm is dropped down into a By Jong (guard position). Since this is an intermediary position flowing immediately into the Jic Gerk front kick at the beginning of section 7, it is not considered a movement within the 116 movements of the Dummy form (*see* Fig 254).

Section 7: Moves 88–99

88. Right Jic Gerk; left Tan Sau, right Wu Sau.
89. Turn left with right Wan Gerk plus right Bong Sau, left Wu Sau.
90. Back to left guard stance.
91. Left Jic Gerk; right Tan Sau, left Wu Sau.
92. Turn right with left Wan Gerk plus left Bong Sau, right Wu Sau.
93. Turn left, right Gum Sau, left Wu Sau.
94. Step 45 degrees, right Huen Ma with low right Wan Jeung, left Pak Sau.
95. Step back in front, turn left Gum Sau, right Wu Sau.
96. Step 45 degrees, left Huen Ma with low left Wan Jeung, right Pak Sau.
97. Step back, Seung Gang Sau at approximately 45 degrees to Dummy in a neutral stance.
98. Face, right Kao Sau, left Jum Sau.
99. Left Jut Sau, right Jic Jeung.

88. Face the Dummy, Right Jic Gerk; Left Tan Sau, Right Wu Sau

From a neutral stance facing the Dummy with a right-hand lead and left Wu Sau (By Jong), bring the left foot, which is to be the supporting leg, into the centreline directly in front of the Dummy, transferring all the weight on to the left leg. Then bring the right (kicking) leg in front of the supporting leg and drive a right Jic Gerk upwards and forwards into the Dummy's body, striking with the centre of the heel approximately half-way

between the Dummy's leg and low, middle arm. At the same time, drive the left Tan Sau forward up and along the centreline to contact with the left Dummy arm, whilst the right arm forms a Wu Sau. The Tan Sau and the Jic Gerk should make contact with the Dummy at the same time.

Jic Gerk, or Jic Tek as it is also known, is a thrusting front kick used at close quarters. Offensively the kick is usually applied when in contact with the opponent's arms or as soon as contact has been gained; defensively it can be used to jam an opponent's kick or as a counter-kick to the opponent's supporting leg.

The kicking leg is quickly brought in front of the body, with toes and knee turned across the centreline just as it leaves the ground. Immediately the knee/leg then rotates outwards whilst the heel of the foot remains on the centreline as it rises. The kick is lifted at the knee, and the foot thrust diagonally upward and forward, though not to full extension, to strike the Dummy on the centreline.

Adhering to the principle, 'The shortest distance between two points is a straight line', the Jic Gerk is driven up and along the centreline (Tse M Seen) directly towards the Dummy (or an opponent) and rises as it travels.

In Wing Chun, Newton's 'Third Law of Motion' can be applied to the fact that when the Jic Gerk strikes the Dummy (or opponent), the Dummy's body is hitting the kicking leg with exactly the same force and that force must go somewhere, hopefully into the opponent. Any resultant force of that impact will be directed down towards the ground and the supporting leg/foot if the kick is applied correctly.

Jic Gerk uses a short, sharp contraction of the quadriceps to create a powerful short-range stamping action using the centre of the heel to deliver the blow, which can be aimed

Fig 255   Right Jic Gerk; left Tan Sau, right Wu Sau.

Fig 256   Turn left with right Wan Gerk plus right Bong Sau, left Wu Sau.

Fig 257   Back to left guard stance.

Fig 258   Left Jic Gerk; right Tan Sau, left Wu Sau.

Fig 259   Turn right with left Wan Gerk plus left Bong Sau, right Wu Sau.

Fig 260   Turn left, right Gum Sau, left Wu Sau.

to the shin, knee, groin or even the lower abdomen of the opponent. It is imperative not to 'chamber' the kick – retract the foot in order to try to develop more power. The foot should always be ahead of the knee, so that it can be used effectively and efficiently from the moment it leaves the ground. Should the foot be chambered in an attempt to increase

Fig 261   Step 45 degrees, right Huen Ma with low right Wan Jeung, left Pak Sau.

Fig 262   Step back in front, turn left Gum Sau, right Wu Sau.

Fig 263   Step 45 degrees, left Huen Ma with low left Wan Jeung, right Pak Sau.

Fig 264   Step back, Seung Gang Sau at approximately 45 degrees to Dummy in a neutral stance.

Fig 265   Face, right Kao Sau, left Jum Sau.

Fig 266   Left Jut Sau, right Jic Jeung.

the power of the kick, it is possible for an opponent at close proximity to quickly step in and jam the kick, trapping the chambered leg and foot as it retracts, leaving the Wing Chun practitioner trapped, vulnerable and off balance.

Immediately travelling forward with the kick may not feel powerful but, in order to

107

be effective, any strike must be able to be delivered. Retracting a strike prior to delivery allows an opponent too much time to respond, counter or simply strike first.

Jic Gerk Checklist

- Always forward the kick from the supporting leg in order to return any impact force to the ground.
- Ensure all the body's mass is located over the supporting leg prior to kicking.

- Do not telegraph the intention to kick by leaning the body or dropping the hands.
- Keep both the supporting leg and the kicking leg bent at the knee.
- Pull the toes and ball of the foot backwards; strike with the centre of the heel.
- The bent knee of the kicking leg should be off the centreline and in front of the hip of the kicking leg.
- The heel and ankle of the kicking leg should be on and controlling the centreline.

CLOCKWISE FROM TOP LEFT:
Fig 267   On guard facing partner.
Fig 268   Opponent punches, counter Jic Gerk, Tan/Wu Sau.
Fig 269   Follow Wan Gerk to knee joint, cover Bong Sau/Wu Sau.
Fig 270   Biu Ma, Jic Kuen.

- The kicking action should be a short, sharp stamp into, but not beyond, the intended target.
- Always kick the closest and easiest accessible target.
- Never kick above waist level.

89. 45-Degree Juen Ma, Right Wan Gerk Plus Right Bong Sau, Left Wu Sau

From the front kick position, pivot on the heel of the supporting (left) leg, angling the hips to approximately 45 degrees, leaning back slightly and applying a right Wan Gerk (stamping sidekick) on to the 'kneecap' of the Dummy's leg. Whilst angling the body to apply the Wan Gerk, rotate the right arm anticlockwise from the Wu Sau position, lifting the elbow and forwarding the forearm to form a Bong Sau. At the same time, retract the Tan Sau below the forming Bong Sau and forward as a Wu Sau to support the Bong Sau (*see* Fig 256).

In application, Wan Gerk can be used either to intercept an opponent's front kick or to counter a front punch by stamping on an opponent's knee joint or just below the knee on the shin (*see* Fig 272). Wan Gerk applied just below the knee can cause a hyperextension injury; the forcible backward bending can cause damage to a number of structures including the bones (contusion), one or both cruciate ligaments, the fat pad, the popliteus tendon or the meniscus. If the kick strikes on to the kneecap, it can cause a patella fracture. Any or all of these injuries can render the opponent incapacitated.

90. Face Dummy, Left By Jong, Right Wu Sau

From the Wan Gerk, turn and face the Dummy in a neutral stance, driving the left Wu Sau forward as By Jong (on-guard stance) and retracting the Bong Sau underneath and forwards as Wu Sau (*see* Fig 257).

Fig 271   On guard facing partner.

Fig 272   Opponent steps in with a punch; counter Wan Tang Gerk, Bong Sau/Wu Sau.

Fig 273   Follow Biu Ma, Jic Kuen/Gum Sau.

CLOCKWISE FROM TOP LEFT:
Fig 274   On guard facing partner.
Fig 275   Opponent throws a front kick; counter Juen Ma, Gum Sau/Wu Sau.
Fig 276   Sharply press Gum Sau, forcing opponent's foot to the floor.
Fig 277   Follow Jic Gerk to back of the knee from behind.
Fig 278   Follow Biu Ma, Chair Pie.

91. Face Dummy, Left Jic Gerk; Right Tan Sau, Left Wu Sau

This is a mirrored repeat of movement 88 (*see* Fig 258).

92. 45-Degree Juen Ma, Left Wan Gerk Plus Left Bong Sau, Right Wu Sau

This is a mirrored repeat of movement 89 (*see* Fig 259).

93. 45-Degree Juen Ma, Right Gum Sau, Left Wu Sau

Place the right leg back on the floor, angling the hips and positioning all the body's mass over the right leg. As the right leg lands on the floor, the right Wu Sau is thrust diagonally down and forwards as Gum Sau to contact (using the heel of the palm) on the low, middle Dummy's arm. Simultaneously, the left Bong Sau is retracted and forwarded

CLOCKWISE FROM TOP LEFT:
Fig 279   On guard facing partner.
Fig 280   Opponent punches; counter 45-degree Biu Man, Pak Sau cover.
Fig 281   Huen Ma behind opponent's lead leg, Jic Jeung/Pak Sau.
Fig 282   Quickly straighten Huen Ma leg, drive Jic Jeung into jaw with Pak Sau to elbow.

as Wu Sau to cover the throat area (*see* Fig 260).

In application, this can be utilized on to the outside gate of an opponent's lead punch or on to the outside gate of an opponent's front kick, at the knee joint. At first, the use of Gum Sau against a front kick seems to contradict the Wing Chun maxim:

> Hand against hand, foot against foot, there is no unstoppable technique.

However, the footwork actually defends against the kick, by safely repositioning the body away from the kick. The Gum Sau makes light contact to the outside face of the attacker's knee, and then a short, sharp energy is applied, driving the leg to the ground (*see* Figs 276 and 277). The utilization of Gum Sau in this way puts the attacker into an awkward position, leaving them extremely vulnerable to counterattack.

Fig 283   Close-up of Huen Ma position prior to application of energy.

Fig 284   Close-up of Huen Ma on to opponent's Achilles tendon.

94. Step 45 Degrees, Right Huen Ma with Right Mid-Level Wan Jeung, Left Wu Sau

Step 45 degrees and circle (Huen Ma) the right leg around and then 'under' the Dummy's leg, placing the ball of the right foot firmly on the floor beneath the Dummy's leg, whilst maintaining contact with the calf (gastrocnemius muscle) on to the underside of the Dummy's leg (*see* Fig 261).

At the same time as performing the Huen Ma step, simultaneously position a Wu Sau cover to the outside of the left Dummy arm and a mid-level Wan Jeung (side palm strike) to the Dummy's body. As the Wan Jeung is applied using a short, sharp wrist snap, the right leg is sharply straightened, driving the heel to the floor. The Wu Sau is pressed on to

the upper left Dummy arm to 'control' the Dummy's arm, which in this instance represents an opponent's elbow.

In a combat application, the Huen Ma can be used to destroy an opponent's stance, body posture and musculoskeletal structure. The 'strike' is used to prevent an opponent moving forward and putting more weight on to their lead leg, therefore diminishing the effect of the Huen Ma, as well as to cause pain or damage. Huen Ma can be applied effectively against either a front kick or a front punch (*see* Fig 281).

A variation of the application of Huen Ma is to stamp down on to the opponent's Achilles tendon (*see* Fig 284), rendering them incapable of standing, let alone continuing any further attack.

Fig 285   On guard facing partner.

Fig 286   Opponent punches; counter 45-degree Biu Ma, Biu Sau/Wu Sau.

Fig 287   Biu Ma trapping the foot, Gum Sau/Wan Jeung.

Fig 288   Sharply rotate the opponent's neck, controlling the jaw and tucking the elbow behind the shoulder.

Fig 289   Sharply pull with Man Geng Sau and knee.

Fig 290   Follow with Chair Pie to the face.

95. Step Back in Front; Juen Ma, Left Gum Sau, Right Wu Sau

Step back in front of the Dummy, angling the hips at 45 degrees, whilst positioning all the body's mass over the left leg. Simultaneously drive the left Gum Sau diagonally down and forwards to contact (using the heel of the palm) on to the low, middle Dummy arm,

Fig 291 On guard facing partner.

Fig 292 Opponent launches a kick; counter Biu Ma 45 degrees to avoid.

Fig 293 Huen Ma behind opponent's leg as it lands, Gwoy Jarn/Wu Sau.

Fig 294 Follow with straightened leg, apply Gwoy Jarn/Wu Sau.

Fig 295 Step back and begin Man Geng Sau/Wu Sau.

Fig 296 Follow with Man Geng Sau and knee strike.

whilst the right hand is forwarded as Wu Sau to cover the throat area (*see* Fig 262).

Gum Sau can be used against a kick, as illustrated earlier, or against a punch where Gum Sau is used to pin the arm whilst pressing into the opponent's hips, affecting their posture, stance and their ability to counter strike (*see* Fig 287).

96. Step 45 Degrees; Left Huen Ma with Low Left Wan Jeung, Right Wu Sau

This is a mirror repeat of movement 94. Huen Ma can just as easily be used to counter a kick as it can to counter a punch (*see* Figs 293 and 294).

97. Seung Gang Sau

Step into a neutral stance (50:50 weight distribution) at approximately a 45-degree angle to the Dummy with Seung Gang Sau (*see* Fig 264). The high Gang Sau arm drives forward to make contact with the Dummy's arm with the inner/upper part of the forearm, about half-way along the ulna and flexor carpi ulnaris muscle, with the elbow pulled in close to the practitioner's centreline. Simultaneously, the lower Gang Sau forwards and connects with the lower, centre arm of the Dummy with the heel of the right palm. The low Gang Sau is similar in shape and structure to the Dai Bong Sau practised in Chum Kiu. If the body position is correct when stepping with the double Gang Sau, then both arms will be in contact with the Dummy's arms with the correct vertical body posture, shoulders relaxed and a strong neutral stance (*see* Fig 264). Simultaneously, the lower Gang Sau forwards and connects with the lower, centre arm of the Dummy with the heel of the right palm.

98. Face, Right Kao Sau, Left Jum Sau

From the Gang Sau step to face the Dummy in a neutral stance, maintaining contact with the high right Gang Sau and circling counter-clockwise to form Kau Sau, as detailed previously. The step and the hip turn together create a short, sharp retraction as the Kau Sau forms, at the same time the low Gang Sau cuts upwards and up the centreline towards the 'head' of the Dummy. Since the Dummy's arms are fixed in position, the left arm is 'intercepted' by the Dummy's arm and therefore converts into Jum Sau on to

the outside of the Dummy's arm, contacting with the inner/upper part of the forearm (*see* Fig 265).

99. Left Jut Sau, Right Jic Jeung

As soon as the left Jum Sau makes contact with the Dummy's arm, it converts to Jut Sau. At the same time, the Kau Sau elbow rolls into the centreline and then drives up the centreline to strike above the Dummy's arms with Jic Jeung, remaining relaxed until fingertip contact, then snapping the wrist forward to apply a sharp palm strike and then immediately relaxing again (*see* Fig 266).

Section 8: Moves 100–116

100. 45-Degree Juen Ma, right Dai Bong Sau, left Wu Sau.
101. 45-Degree Juen Ma, left Dai Bong Sau, right Wu Sau.
102. 45-Degree Juen Ma, right Dai Bong Sau, left Wu Sau.
103. Face, right Tan Sau/left Wu Sau to right Wan Jeung.
104. 45-Degree Juen Ma, left Dai Bong Sau, right Wu Sau.
105. Face, left Tan Sau/right Wu Sau to right Wan Jeung.
106. 45-Degree Juen Ma, right Gum Sau, left Wu Sau.
107. Step 45 degrees, left Pak Sau, right Wu Sau plus right 45-degree Jic Gerk to knee.
108. Step back, 45-degree Juen Ma, left Gum Sau, right Wu Sau.
109. Step 45 degrees, right Pak Sau, left Wu Sau plus left 45-degree Jic Gerk to knee.
110. Step back, 45-degree Juen Ma, right Bong Sau, left Wu Sau.
111. 45-Degree Juen Ma, Seung Lap Sau and right Pak Gerk to shin.
112. 45-Degree Juen Ma, left Bong Sau, right Wu Sau.

Fig 297   45-Degree Juen Ma, right Dai Bong Sau, left Wu Sau.

Fig 298   45-Degree Juen Ma, left Dai Bong Sau, right Wu Sau.

Fig 299   45-Degree Juen Ma, right Dai Bong Sau, left Wu Sau.

Figs 300   Face, right Tan Sau/left Wu Sau to right Wan Jeung.

Fig 301   45-Degree Juen Ma, left Dai Bong Sau, right Wu Sau.

113. 45-Degree Juen Ma, Seung Lap Sau and left Pak Gerk to shin.
114. Step back, Gang Sau at approximately 45 degrees to Dummy.
115. Face, right Kao Sau, left Jum Sau.
116. Left Jut Sau, right Jic Jeung.

Figs 302   Face, left Tan Sau/right Wu Sau to right Wan Jeung.

Fig 303   45-Degree Juen Ma, right Gum Sau, left Wu Sau.

Fig 304   Step 45 degrees, left Pak Sau, right Wu Sau plus right 45-degree Jic Gerk to knee.

Fig 305   Step back, 45-degree Juen Ma, left Gum Sau, right Wu Sau.

Fig 306   Step 45 degrees, right Pak Sau, left Wu Sau plus left 45-degree Jic Gerk to knee.

100. 45-Degree Juen Ma, Right Dai Bong Sau, Left Wu Sau

From the right Jic Jeung retract, lower and rotate the forearm anticlockwise to form Dai Bong Sau, and then forward the Dai Bong Sau in conjunction with a left Wu Sau and a 45-degree turning stance (Juen Ma). Dai Bong Sau uses the flat of the forearm

117

CLOCKWISE FROM TOP LEFT:
Fig 307   Step back, 45-degree Juen Ma, right Bong Sau, left Wu Sau.
Fig 308   45-Degree Juen Ma, Seung Lap Sau and right Pak Gerk to shin.
Fig 309   45-Degree Juen Ma, left Bong Sau, right Wu Sau.
Fig 310   45-Degree Juen Ma, Seung Lap Sau and left Pak Gerk to shin.
Fig 311   Step back, Gang Sau at approximately 45 degrees to Dummy.

to connect with the low, middle Dummy arm; this prevents over-rotating the forearm, which would put pressure on the shoulder joint, and it ensures contact on the muscle groups (extensor carpi ulnaris, extensor digiti minimi and extensor digitorum) rather than hitting along the ulna bone (*see* Fig 297).

Dai Bong Sau can be applied against either a mid-level thrusting punch or a thrusting kick. It is used to deflect the strike and then return quickly to the centreline (*see* Fig 316).

101. 45-Degree Juen Ma, Left Dai Bong Sau, Right Wu Sau

From the right Dai Bong Sau retract, raise and rotate the forearm clockwise to form Wu Sau; at the same time forward, lower and rotate the forearm to form a left Dai Bong Sau. Forward the Dai Bong Sau in conjunction with a right

LEFT: Fig 312 Face, right Kao Sau, left Jum Sau.
RIGHT: Fig 313 Left Jut Sau, right Jic Jeung.

Wu Sau and a 45-degree turning stance (Juen Ma) (*see* Fig 298).

102. 45-Degree Juen Ma, Right Dai Bong Sau, Left Wu Sau

From the left Dai Bong Sau retract, raise and rotate the forearm clockwise to form Wu Sau; at the same time forward, lower and rotate the forearm to form a left Dai Bong Sau. Dai Bong Sau, in conjunction with a left Wu Sau and a 45-degree turning stance (Juen Ma), is forwarded into the Dummy (*see* Fig 299).

Fig 314 On guard facing opponent.

Fig 315 Opponent punches; counter Juen Ma, Dai Bong Sau/Wu Sau.

Fig 316 Follow Lap Sau, Fak Sau (half move shown to counter second punch). *(Sequence continued on page 120.)*

(Cont. from page 119.)
Fig 317   Lap Sau, Fak Sau.

Fig 318   Step in Gwoy Jarn, Gum Sau.

Fig 319   Follow with Fak Sau/ Wu Sau.

103. Face, Right Tan Sau/Left Wu Sau to Right Wan Jeung

Turn into a neutral stance, facing the Dummy. From the right Dai Bong Sau, forward, raise and 'corkscrew' the forearm clockwise up and along the centreline to form Tan Sau, applying a continuous forward energy from the elbow towards the centre of the Dummy's body, whilst maintaining the left Wu Sau to cover the throat area (*see* Figs 300). The Tan Sau structure in this instance is a transitional position used to control the centreline and therefore the opponent; the arm immediately drives up and along the centreline, rotating it anticlockwise to form Wan Jeung. It is important to ensure that the centre of the heel of the palm (in line with the radius and ulna) lightly contacts the Dummy at first, then the energy, driven by the elbow, is sharply snapped into the centre of the Dummy. It is equally important to relax quickly again, keeping the fingertips lightly in contact with the Dummy's body as it 'rocks' due to the applied energy.

The Tan Sau to an immediate strike movement can be applied equally on the inside gate and outside gate.

104. 45-Degree Juen Ma, Left Dai Bong Sau

This is a mirrored repeat of movement 102 (*see* Fig 301).

105. Face, Left Tan Sau/Right Wu Sau to Right Wan Jeung

This is a mirrored repeat of movement 103 (*see* Figs 302).

106. 45-Degree Juen Ma, Right Gum Sau, Left Wu Sau

Turn sharply at 45 degrees, twisting and angling the hips, as the right Wu Sau is driven diagonally down and forwards as Gum Sau to contact (using the heel of the palm) on the low, middle Dummy arm. Simultaneously, the left Wan Jeung is retracted and forwarded as Wu Sau to cover the throat area (*see* Fig 303).

Fig 320   On guard facing opponent.

Fig 321   Opponent punches; counter Juen Ma, Dai Bong Sau/Wu Sau.

Fig 322   Opponent punches again; counter Juen Ma, Tan Da.

Fig 323   Follow Gum Sau/ Wan Jeung.

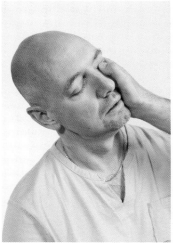

Fig 324   Close-up of thumb in the eye, shown from alternative angle.

Fig 325   Follow with Juen Ma, Jic Kuen/Gum Sau.

As discussed and illustrated previously, Gum Sau can be applied on to the outside gate of an opponent's lead punch or on to the outside gate of an opponent's knee to control a front kick.

107. 45-Degree Bui Ma, Juen Ma; Left Pak Sau, Right Wu Sau Plus Right 45-Degree Jic Gerk to Knee

From the right Gum Sau position, Biu Ma parallel to the Dummy and then Juen Ma

Fig 326   On guard facing opponent.
Fig 327   Opponent punches; counter Juen Ma, Dai Bong Sau/Wu Sau.
Fig 328   Opponent punches again; Juen Ma, Jic Gerk to knee, Pak Sau/Wu Sau.
Fig 329   Step in, Gwoy Jarn/Gum Sau.
Fig 330   Turn, Jic Kuen/Gang Sau cover.

to face the Dummy's body whilst applying a left Pak Sau to the left Dummy arm, which in this instance represents the elbow on the outside gate of an opponent's strike. At the same time, drive a right Jic Gerk from the supporting leg to attack the side of the knee of the Dummy's leg, landing at exactly the same moment as the Pak Sau. The left Pak Sau is supported by a right Wu Sau to protect and cover the Wing Chun practitioner's throat area (*see* Fig 304).

The Jic Gerk is applied at 45 degrees to the Dummy's leg, to the top/side of the knee joint for maximum effect and damage (*see* Fig 328).

108. Step Back, Turn Left Gum Sau and Right Wu Sau

Step back in front of the Dummy, angling the hips to 45 degrees and positioning all the body's mass over the left leg. Thrust the left Gum Sau diagonally down and forwards to contact on the low, middle Dummy arm,

CLOCKWISE FROM TOP LEFT:
Fig 331   On guard facing opponent.
Fig 332   Opponent punches; counter Juen Ma, Pak Sau/Wu Sau.
Fig 333   Opponent launches a front kick; counter Biu Ma/Juen Ma.
Fig 334   Jic Gerk to knee as kick lands.
Fig 335   Biu Ma, Jic Kuen/Wu Sau.

using the heel of the palm. Simultaneously, the right hand is forwarded as Wu Sau to cover the throat area (*see* Fig 305).

109. Step 45 Degrees, Juen Ma; Right Pak Sau, Left Wu Sau Plus Left 45-Degree Jic Gerk to Knee

From the left Gum Sau position, Biu Ma parallel to the Dummy and then Juen Ma to face the Dummy's body whilst applying a right Pak Sau to the left Dummy arm, which in this instance represents the elbow on the outside gate of an opponent's strike. At the same time, drive a left Jic Gerk from the supporting leg to attack the side of the knee of the Dummy's leg, landing at exactly the same moment as the Pak Sau. The right Pak Sau is supported by a left Wu Sau to protect and cover the Wing Chun practitioner's throat area (*see* Fig 306).

The Jic Gerk kick can be applied as a counter to an opponent's kick, driving Jic Gerk at 45 degrees to the side of the knee joint just as an opponent's kick lands and a large percentage of their body's mass is placed on their lead knee (*see* Fig 334).

110. Step Back, 45-Degree Juen Ma, Right Bong Chor Sau/Left Wu Sau

Step back in front of the Dummy, twisting and angling the hips, positioning all the body's mass over the right leg. Drive forward a right Bong Sau on to the end of the inside of the left Dummy arm, representing the inside gate of an opponent's wrist, hence Bong Chor Sau. The Bong Chor Sau is supported by a left Wu Sau to cover the throat area (*see* Fig 307).

Bong Chor Sau should be considered an intermediary movement; a transition technique used purely to gain contact and therefore sensory information prior to applying the next technique. As soon as the Bong Chor Sau makes contact, for example, it is possible to ascertain the momentum, direction and energy of the strike, feel when the strike reaches extension, then momentarily pauses, and the moment the arm begins to retract, all skills developed and refined within Chi Sau.

111. 45-Degree Juen Ma, Seung Lap Sau and Right Pak Gerk

Turn (Juen Ma) sharply, angling the hips at 45 degrees whilst maintaining a continuous forward pressure from the elbow. Rotate the Bong Chor Sau clockwise, maintaining wrist contact throughout, and drop the elbow until it represents Biu Sau. At the same time, the Wu Sau travels forward at the wrist to resemble a Tan Sau shape, and then both arms apply a double Lap Sau in conjunction with a right Pak Gerk (*see* Fig 308). Figure 308 shows the position just prior to the application of the Pak Gerk energy.

In reality, the Seung Lap Sau is actually an application of Jip Sau as learnt and practised in Chum Kiu. Jip Sau is a combination of Tok Sau and Jut Sau, which can be used to control/jar the elbow joint or, under extreme circumstances, even break an opponent's arm. To successfully deploy Jip Sau, an initial bridging technique, in this case Bong Chor Sau, is used to find an attacker's arm. However, as soon as contact has been made, the Bong Chor Sau converts to Lap Sau (using Jut Sau energy) to control the attacker's wrist, whilst the rear Wu Sau drives forward to contact and control the attacker's elbow joint. The movements of Seung Lap Sau (Jip Sau), in conjunction with the turning stance, must be short, fast and powerful in order to be effective and protect the upper section of the body. The Wing Chun practitioner's upper wrist is located at the end of the Dummy's arm 'at the wrist', the lower arm positioned close to the Dummy's body 'at the elbow'.

Pak Gerk is a short, sharp heel strike on to the front of the Dummy leg's 'shin', timed to coincide with the double Lap Sau (*see* Fig 338).

In application, this technique can be applied from a point of contact on the outside gate, should the opponent's strike pause or start to attempt to retract. Upon contact, with Biu Sau for example, turn to 45 degrees (Juen Ma), angling the hips whilst applying a sharp, double Lap Sau to the opponent's arm, controlling both the wrist and the elbow. At the same time, apply a sharp Pak Gerk to the opponent's shin to injure, to cause pain and to cause an imbalance in the opponent's body posture.

112. 45-Degree Juen Ma, Left Bong Sau, Right Wu Sau

Step back in front of the Dummy, twisting and angling the hips, positioning all the body's mass over the left leg. Drive forward a left Bong Sau on to the end of the inside of the right Dummy arm, representing the inside gate of an opponent's wrist, hence Bong Chor Sau. A right Wu Sau to cover the

CLOCKWISE FROM TOP LEFT:
Fig 336   On guard facing opponent.
Fig 337   Opponent punches; Biu Ma, Biu Sau/Wu Sau.
Fig 338   Follow Juen Ma, Seung Lap Sau/Jic Gerk.
Fig 339   Biu Ma, Gwoy Jarn/Gum Sau.
Fig 340   Juen Ma, Jic Kuen/Wu Sau.

throat area (*see* Fig 309) supports Bong Chor Sau.

113. 45-Degree Juen Ma, Seung Lap Sau and Left Pak Gerk

Turn (Juen Ma) sharply, angling the hips at 45 degrees whilst maintaining a continuous forward pressure from the elbow. Rotate the left Bong Chor Sau clockwise, maintaining wrist contact throughout and dropping the elbow until it represents Biu Sau. At the same time, the right Wu Sau travels forward at the wrist to resemble a Tan Sau shape, and then both arms apply a double Lap Sau energy in conjunction with a left Pak Gerk (*see* Fig 310). Figure 310 shows the positions as the Pak Gerk is applied.

114. Seung Gang Sau

The next movement is to step into a neutral stance (50:50 weight distribution) at approximately a 45-degree angle to the Dummy with Seung Gang Sau. The upper Gang Sau arm drives forward to make contact with the

125

CLOCKWISE FROM TOP LEFT:
Fig 341   On guard facing partner.
Fig 342   Opponent launches front kick; counter Seung Gang Sau.
Fig 343   Follow Biu Ma, Jic Kuen/Wu Sau.
Fig 344   Opponent punches again; counter Kau Sau/Jic Kuen.
Fig 345   Follow with Gwoy Jarn/Gum Sau.

Dummy's arm with the inner/upper part of the forearm, about half-way along the ulna and flexor carpi ulnaris muscle, with the elbow pulled in close to the practitioner's centreline. Simultaneously, the lower Gang Sau forwards and connects with the lower, centre arm of the Dummy with the heel of the right palm (*see* Fig 311). The low Gang Sau is similar in shape and structure to the Dai Bong Sau practised in Chum Kiu.

As discussed previously, if the body position is correct when stepping with the double Gang Sau then both arms will be in contact with the Dummy's arms with the correct vertical body posture, shoulders relaxed and a strong neutral stance.

115. Face, Right Kao Sau, Left Jum Sau

From the Gang Sau, step to face the Dummy in a neutral stance, maintaining contact with the high right Gang Sau and then circling counter-clockwise to form Kau Sau, similar to a Bong Sau in shape but controlling the right Dummy arm using the heel of the palm.

Fig 346 Chi Sau: Sifu Shaun Rawcliffe (A) on the left, Sifu John Brogden (B) on the right.

Fig 347 Partner A rolls to Bong Sau/Fook Sau.

Fig 348 Feeling B pushing forward, A turns with Kau Sau/Wu, drawing in partner B.

Fig 349 Partner A turns back to face B forming Po Pai Jeung to control B's arms.

Fig 350 Partner A steps in with Po Pai Jeung to make light initial contact.

Fig 351 Partner A applies Po Pai Jeung energy, off balancing B.

The combination of the step and the hip turn creates a short, sharp retraction as the Kau Sau forms. At the same time, the low Gang Sau cuts upwards on to the outside gate on the left Dummy arm (*see* Fig 312).

In application, the low Gang Sau would probably cut up the centreline and strike the opponent. However, on the Dummy the low Gang Sau travels up the centreline towards the Dummy's 'head' but is 'intercepted' by the Dummy's arm. It therefore converts into Jum Sau on to the outside of the left Dummy arm, contacting with the inner/upper part of the forearm, about half-way along the ulna and flexor carpi ulnaris muscle, with the elbow pulled in close to the practitioner's centreline.

Kau Sau is a very useful tool in Chi Sau when dealing with a forceful opponent. It can be used to 'draw in' and off balance an opponent who is using too much forward force or pushing with their body. The opponent's loss of balance presents the opportunity to apply a strike or controlling technique (*see* Fig 348).

116. Left Jut Sau, Right Jic Jeung

As soon as the left Jum Sau makes contact with the Dummy's arm, it switches to Jut Sau; the Kau Sau elbow quickly drops into the centreline and the arm drives up and along the centreline to strike with Jic Jeung (*see* Fig 313).

As discussed previously, the vertical palm strike is the weapon of choice because its structure means that the elbow is slightly off the centreline and can be used to contact and control the opponent's right punch prior to the palm strike landing. The palm strike should remain relaxed until the fingertips touch the Dummy, then the heel of the palm should be snapped forwards, driven inwards upon contact and immediately relaxed afterwards. This results in a driven energy from contact, rather than a hit, applying energy into, not on to, the Dummy. As the Dummy rocks on its frame due to the energy of the palm strike, the fingertips should remain in contact with the Dummy's body, monitoring its movement.

Mor Jong

Mor – Cantonese term meaning **polish** *tr.*, to make perfect or complete; to study or practise until adept.
Jong – Cantonese term meaning **stake** *n.*, a stick or metal bar driven into the ground.

Having completed learning and refining the sequence and movements of the Dummy form, the next stage is to drill the primary and secondary core techniques within each section. This process is known as Mor Jong and requires the Wing Chun practitioner to practise repeatedly the core techniques of each section in order to facilitate refining and developing the necessary skills required to apply each technique correctly and powerfully, without conscious thought. These automated responses are a result of Mor Jong.

> There is no substitute for mileage.
> *Shaun Rawcliffe*

Any new skill involving coordination requires time and practice until the new combination of movements and muscle contractions required to execute that movement has been learned. Only then can that movement be performed without concentration and conscious effort.

Neuroscientists have long known that learning only takes place when new connections are made between brain nerve cells, and that large parts of the cerebral cortex of the brain are taken up with 'association areas', which analyse and register data received from the primary senses. For example, complex movement sequences are analysed and registered by the premotor cortex, and voluntary movement by the primary motor cortex.

However, without such repeated experience, key synapses do not form, and if such connections, once formed, are not used frequently enough to be strengthened or reinforced, the brain, figuring they are no longer required, eventually 'prunes' them away. The more times that patterns of thought are repeated, the quicker that information will be recalled. It is analogous to walking through an overgrown field. Initially, you have to fight your way through the undergrowth. If you do not travel that path again, it will quickly become overgrown and you may not even realize that you have been down the path. If, however, you continually travel along that path, eventually it will turn into a recognizable track, then a footpath, which may turn into a lane, or even a road.

However, repetition alone is not sufficient to remember a movement, or combination of movements. The sensations and musculoskeletal structures required to perform those movements must be transferred into the motor areas of the brain and stored in the long-term memory. This process, known as consolidation, requires attention, repetition and associative ideas. With constant practice, the neural networks and motor neuron/muscle group pathways become fast and effortless, requiring no conscious thought to achieve the fluid sequence of motor activity that produces the desired action or actions. This is sometimes referred to as 'muscle memory', and is the terminology used to describe the phenomenon of skeletal muscle activity that is learned and becomes essentially automatic with practice.

In order to provide a more insightful and accurate reflection of drilling and learning methodology, I have included below an article written by one of my students, Genea Nicole Rawcliffe:

Learning and Mor Jong: A rationale presented by Genea Nicole Rawcliffe

Introduction

> … learning is done by people, not to them.
> *(Race, 2007, p. 26)*

As the mother of a young child, the question, 'Why?' is a frequently occurring and often grating annoyance that emanates from an innocent, inexperienced vessel, craving to be filled with knowledge and understanding. So much so, that I have to remind myself of my late Granddad's 'words of wisdom' and quite possibly the best advice I have ever been given: 'If you are ever unsure about anything, you must ask questions.' Yet as a Wing Chun practitioner, it is I who have become the vessel, and the thirst for knowledge and understanding has a long-established place in my own training and, I suspect, in the training of other practitioners. Effective questioning is *key* to learning and to developing, and it is with an all-embracing and encouraging attitude to those who may ask, *'Why?'*, that I shall examine the following:

- How do we learn effectively?
- Why is drilling so important in a training regime?
- How can drilling facilitate the learning process?

Education, to my mind, is a partnership between the facilitator of learning and the learner. The responsibility of the facilitator is to motivate and inspire the learner, and the responsibility of the learner is to make the choice to learn and develop through hard work and commitment. The nurturing and development of this partnership, I believe, is intrinsic to the establishment of an effective teaching and learning environment. Race

129

(2007) clearly highlights the responsibilities of both the learner and the facilitator of learning, and it is with recognition of these key ideas that I seek to consider the place of learning within the Wing Chun system and the value of drilling (Mor Jong).

Effective Learning and Mor Jong

> **Learn** *v* **learning**, **learnt** *or* **learned**. 1, Gain skill or knowledge by study, practice, or teaching. 2, Memorize (something). 3, Find out or discover.
>
> *(HarperCollins, 1996, p. 287)*

There are many schools of thought regarding the meaning of 'learning', which are too numerous to mention in this article. However, worthy of note and arguably more relevant to the issue of effective learning, is the work of Race (2007), in which he defines five factors that can underpin *successful* learning:

1. *Wanting*: motivation, interest, enthusiasm.
2. *Needing*: necessity, survival, saving face.
3. *Doing*: practice, repetition, experience, trial and error.
4. *Feedback*: other people's reactions, seeing the results.
5. *Digesting*: making sense of what has been learned.

Whatever the motivational factor, undoubtedly several of these elements link specifically to learning, drilling and training Wing Chun.

In order for effective learning to take place, the learner needs to take responsibility for his or her own learning, as asserted above, and in doing so, question *why* something is done. This, of course, may be representative of the *wanting* or *needing* elements of Race's model. However, it is the *questioning* that can

facilitate the learning experience, through a thorough analysis of what is being demonstrated and its purpose, both within the Wing Chun system and in 'real-life' scenarios. Similarly, as an instructor, a thorough understanding of purpose is essential, and effective answers, perhaps delivered through demonstration and explanation, need to be communicated in a way that caters for a variety of learning styles. In addition, the instructor's responsibility to assess knowledge, skills and understanding is paramount here, coupled with the provision of effective *feedback*, again identified in Race's model, in order to support and develop the Wing Chun practitioner.

It is with the assumption that these elements are secure, that I now examine the importance of drilling in personal training. 'Mimicking' is an activity with which the Wing Chun practitioner frequently engages – copying the sequence of movements that have been demonstrated by the instructor – but it is the *interaction* with and *understanding* of those movements, coupled with the *commitment* of the learner, that pave the way to consolidation, acquisition of knowledge and skills and the potential generation of new questions. Here, the *doing* and *digesting* elements in Race's model surface. As stated previously, choosing to work hard and to commit are key, if one is to develop as a Wing Chun practitioner.

This interaction, repetition and consequently a development in understanding of the key movements of the Wing Chun Wooden Dummy encourage the learner to:

• Commit to 'head' memory the accurate positioning and structure, sequential movements and the intricacies of moving between those movements. This committal will allow the practitioner to remember and, therefore, practise from memory.

- Commit to 'body' memory or 'muscle' memory the positioning and structure, sequential movements and the intricacies of moving between those movements. This committal will allow the body to respond in a dependable, conditioned way.

Both rely on repetition as the key to effective learning and, therefore, efficient deployment of the 'tool' or position at the correct time. However, that is not to say that all learners will necessarily progress at the same rate, or benefit solely by this *kinaesthetic* approach to learning, as I will now examine.

Learning Styles and Mor Jong

Learning by 'doing' (kinaesthetic learning), learning by 'seeing' (visual learning) and learning by 'listening' (auditory learning) are all different 'learning styles' and each individual may have their own dominant style. You may wish to examine what kind of a learner you are; for example, one practitioner may learn more readily if allowed to listen to and consequently learn from explanations of how to apply movements on the dummy (predominantly an auditory learner); another may choose to observe the movements being drilled and learn in a visual way (predominantly a visual learner); another may gain more from being given the opportunity to physically engage with the dummy, or by drilling each movement 'in the air' – learning from 'doing' (predominantly a kinaesthetic learner). Some practitioners may use a combination of all three, in differing quantities (multi-modal learning). The peripheral visual and auditory learning experiences that occur at the time of physical demonstration and student interaction will be relevant in varying capacities to each individual, but it is an understanding of the *partnership* between these learning experiences that will ensure greater success. Identification of your

own learning style is helpful when training Wing Chun, as it allows you to focus more readily on those areas that may have greater meaning for you as an individual and may, in turn, provide the opportunity to achieve greater success in Wing Chun learning.

Additionally, recognition that 'rates of learning' differ from learner to learner is also of great importance and could impact greatly upon self-esteem, which in turn could impact upon your success in training. Recognition of these elements is crucial when training with a partner, small group or individual who may learn in a very different way to you.

The Benefits of Mor Jong

Understanding and embracing your own learning style and pace could facilitate learning, although it is important to identify that it is the *kinaesthetic* aspect of physically drilling each individual movement that will allow muscle memory to develop and that could contribute to success on the dummy. Wing Chun is, after all, a martial art that involves physically engaging with the 'toolkit'. There is no substitute for repetition of physical movements, and it is this 'drilling' that could lead to a more coherent comprehension of the movements, sequence and applications of the dummy form. The absence of drilling and, more specifically, *regular drilling*, in my experience can lead to weaknesses further down the line, with key concepts and movements being forgotten and undertrained. Returning for a moment to the dictionary definition of learning, I would argue that the 'study', 'practice' and (eventually, when equipped) 'teaching' elements are those that allow a development in skills and knowledge. The conscious repetition of correct position, posture, energy and sequencing provides the foundations upon which successful (and potentially devastating) movements can be built upon, developed further and refined.

Mor Jong can:

- improve speed, accuracy, reflexes, coordination, position and structure
- allow head and muscle memory to develop
- provide opportunities for self-correction
- provide more opportunities for physical conditioning, stamina and can promote a healthy body and mind
- consolidate learning.

Furthermore, I would advocate that Mor Jong is a vehicle through which greater success in Wing Chun can be achieved. Indubitably, it involves repetition, time and dedication if it is to be successful and, if adopted by the Wing Chun practitioner, the reward will be an improved, polished performance. In a bona fide combat scenario, the latter is invaluable and may be the difference between injury or safety, life or death. My Granddad was a man of very few words, yet his words live on and may even contribute to saving lives.

Now ask yourself again: 'Why?'

Acknowledgements

Thank you to Scott Buckler, a friend, colleague and fellow Midlands Wing Chun Kuen practitioner and instructor, for his unwavering support and for his valuable insight into learning theory. Thanks also to my teacher and mentor, Sifu Rawcliffe, for providing equal opportunities for all to engage in Wing Chun and for motivating and guiding a new generation of successful Wing Chun practitioners into the twenty-first century.

Genea Nicole Rawcliffe MA, BA, QTS trains at the Solihull branch of the Midlands Wing Chun Kuen under the supervision of Sifu Rawcliffe.

She has a BA (Hons) in Primary Teaching and an MA with Distinction in Education. Currently, Genea is employed as a teacher at a primary school in Birmingham and as a lecturer at the University of Worcester.

Core Techniques of the First and Second Sections

Bong Sau to Tan Sau/Wan Jeung

The primary core technique of both the first and second sections of the Dummy are the Bong Sau to Tan Sau/Wan Jeung movements applied whilst stepping around the Dummy's leg and repositioning at approximately 45 degrees. The Bong Sau to Tan Sau to Bong Sau to Tan Sau movements need to be practised until the footwork and hand transitions are smooth and effortless. The Bong Sau should flow into the Tan Sau, maintaining a constant energy from the elbow, along the arm, through the Dummy's arm and into the body. The footwork should be fluid and powerful, moving around the Dummy's leg and then stepping in to make firm and deliberate contact with the side of the Dummy's leg at exactly the same time as the Tan Sau and Wan Jeung make contact with the arm and body of the Dummy (*see* Fig 354).

When moving to the opposite side of the Dummy, the Bong Sau should roll over the Dummy's arm and then forward until the Bong Sau makes light contact with the last few inches of the Dummy's arm (*see* Fig 355). The Bong Sau then applies a continuous pressure forwards via the contact point on the Dummy's arm, into the centre of the Dummy and then smoothly flows into the Tan Sau/Wan Jeung as discussed above (*see* Fig 357).

Fig 352   Bong Sau to left Dummy arm.

Fig 353   Step and half movement from Tan Sau to Bong Sau.

Fig 354   Tan Sau/Wan Jeung and foot contact to Dummy's leg.

Fig 355   Biu Ma Bong Sau to right Dummy arm.

Fig 356   Step and half movement from Tan Sau to Bong Sau.

Fig 357   Tan Sau/Wan Jeung and foot contact to Dummy's leg and repeat.

Key points

- Maintain a forwarding energy from the elbow, through the wrist into the centre of the Dummy upon contact.
- Do not clash with the Dummy's arm when applying Bong Sau or Wan Jeung; make light contact and then apply forward energy.

133

CLOCKWISE FROM TOP LEFT:
Fig 358   Tan Sau/Wan Jeung and foot contact to Dummy's leg.
Fig 359   Seung Gang Sau at approximately 45 degrees.
Fig 360   Biu Ma Kwun Sau.
Fig 361   Step and half movement from Tan Sau to Bong Sau.
Fig 362   Tan Sau/Wan Jeung and foot contact to Dummy's leg and repeat.

- Stick to the Dummy's arm whilst rolling from Bong Sau to Tan Sau.
- Look forward at the 'head' of the Dummy; do not look at your feet.
- Always ensure three points of contact: Tan Sau, Wan Jeung and the foot.
- Take short, powerful steps and circle the foot, staying close to the Dummy's leg, before stepping in and making contact with the side of the foot/shin.

- Maintain a good vertical posture, correct stance width and the necessary musculoskeletal structure in the arms.

Tan Sau/Wan Jeung to Seung Gang Sau to Kwun Sau

The secondary core drill is to add Seung Gang Sau (*see* Fig 359) and Kwun Sau (*see* Fig 360) into the above sequence, in other words Tan Sau to Seung Gang Sau to Kwun Sau to Tan Sau.

This drill practises and refines moving and flowing from Seung Gang Sau to Kwun Sau in order to identify and instil the similarities and the differences in structure, energy and body positioning between the two techniques. The drill enhances the ability to smoothly flow from the Dai Bong Sau position (part of Kwun Sau) to the high Tan Sau (*see* Figs 360–362), reinforcing the process of disengaging contact from the low Dummy arm and quickly re-establishing contact on the upper Dummy arm by taking the shortest and most direct path possible, avoiding retracting the arms unnecessarily and therefore making hard impact upon re-engaging contact. Both the Seung Gang Sau and the Kwun Sau should use forward energy upon contact into the centre of the Dummy, and not clash with the Dummy's arms by pushing across them.

Key points

- Maintain a forwarding energy from the elbows, through the wrist into the centre of the Dummy upon contact.
- Do not clash with the Dummy's arm when applying either Seung Gang Sau or Kwun Sau; make light contact and then apply forward energy into the Dummy.
- Look forward at the 'head' of the Dummy; do not look at your feet.
- Seung Gang Sau utilizes a neutral stance (50:50 weight distribution) at an angle to the Dummy.
- Kwun Sau utilizes a short, sharp Biu Ma step, with the majority of the weight on the rear leg, parallel to the Dummy.
- Take short, powerful steps and circle the foot, staying close to the Dummy's leg, before stepping in and making contact with the side of the foot/shin.

- A good vertical posture, correct stance width and the necessary musculoskeletal structure in the arms are essential.

Core Techniques of the Third Section

Pak Sau to Fak Sau to Gum Sau/Jic Kuen

One of the core techniques of the third section of the Dummy is the Pak Sau to Fak Sau to Gum Sau/Jic Kuen. This drill improves speed, reflexes and fluidity as well as the ability to switch quickly and smoothly from one energy and direction to another.

The Pak Sau/Juen Ma to Fak Sau movement requires practise until it is fast, fluid and powerful. As soon as Pak Sau applies the short, sharp energy into the Dummy's arm (*see* Fig 363), it drives forward as Fak Sau to 'strike' the 'neck' area of the Dummy (*see* Fig 364). There should be hardly any pause between the application of the Pak Sau and the initiation of the Fak Sau. Pak Sau should almost be a half move, pulling in slightly upon contact, as if in application trying to pass the punch past the practitioner's right shoulder, then immediately flowing into Fak Sau, which makes light initial contact with the Dummy and then drives the energy into the centre of the Dummy (Fak Da). As soon as the Fak Sau applies the energy into the Dummy, relax and turn to face the Dummy with a left Gum Sau and a right mid-level punch (*see* Fig 365), and then continue the drill by repeating the equivalent movements on the opposite side (*see* Figs 366–368).

Key points

- Do not collide forcefully with the Dummy's arm when applying Fak Sau; make light contact and then apply forward energy.

Fig 363　Juen Ma, Pak Sau/ Wu Sau.

Fig 364　Fak Da/Wu Sau.

Fig 365　Gum Sau/Jic Kuen.

Fig 366　Juen Ma, Pak Sau/ Wu Sau.

Fig 367　Fak Da/Wu Sau.

Fig 368　Gum Sau/Jic Kuen and repeat.

- Look forward at the 'head' of the Dummy; do not look down.
- Do not apply excessive force with Pak Sau; apply the appropriate energy then quickly flow into Fak Sau.
- Do not make hard contact with the Jic Kuen.
- When applying the Gum Sau, pull downwards and inwards sharply.

CLOCKWISE FROM TOP LEFT:
Fig 369 Juen Ma, Dai
Bong Sau/Wu Sau.
Fig 370 Step around and
in with Fak Da/Pak Sau.
Fig 371 Step back, Wan
Gerk/Bong Sau/Wu Sau.
Fig 372 Step Biu Ma, Dai
Bong Sau to continue the
drill.

- Maintain a good vertical posture, correct stance width and the necessary musculoskeletal structure in the arms.

Dai Bong Sau, Biu Ma/ Fak Sau to Wan Gerk

Another core technique of the third section of the Dummy is the Dai Bong Sau, Biu Ma/ Fak Sau to Wan Gerk sequence. When drilling this sequence, pay particular attention to

the stepping footwork and the distance and body posture when kicking. When moving from the Dai Bong Sau to the Fak Sau, do not draw back the Dai Bong Sau arm for power; it should retract just enough to clear the low Dummy arm and then immediately drive the Fak Sau forwards into the Dummy's body as the body is repositioned (*see* Fig 370). When applying the Fak Sau, the weight need not be positioned fully over the rear leg; it may even be evenly distributed (50:50 weight distribution), but then the body mass must be relocated on to the rear leg in order to apply the Wan Gerk (*see* Fig 371). The Wan Gerk kicking leg is then quickly driven back to the floor as a Biu Ma step in order to apply the Dai Bong Sau (*see* Fig 372), and then the drill is continued by repeating the equivalent movements on the opposite side of the Dummy.

Key points

- Do not clash with the Dummy's arm when applying Dai Bong Sau; make light contact and then apply forward energy into the Dummy along the Dummy's arm.
- Look forward at the 'head' of the Dummy; do not look down.
- Do not apply excessive force with the Fak Sau or the simultaneous Pak Sau; apply the appropriate energy upon contact with the Dummy's body.
- Maintain a good posture, slightly leaning back with all the weight over the supporting leg when kicking.
- When applying Wan Gerk, make light contact on the Dummy's body with the toes, and then apply a short, sharp stamp through the heel diagonally downwards.
- Do not over-rotate the knee and hip when kicking; lift the kick at the knee and angle the knee and foot to a maximum of 45 degrees.
- Maintain a good vertical posture, correct stance width and the necessary musculoskeletal structure in the arms in Dai Bong Sau; do not lean forward.

Core Techniques of the Fourth Section

Kau Sau/Jum Sau

Drilling the Kau Sau/Jum Sau sequence improves speed, reflexes and fluidity as well as the ability to stick to and control an opponent. This drill should be practised in conjunction with a Juen Ma (turning) stance to coordinate the hand and stance work.

The drill can begin from a Seung Gang Sau position, rolling into a right Kau Sau/left Jum Sau (*see* Fig 373). As the right Kau Sau rolls anticlockwise under the Dummy's arm, maintaining contact throughout the movement, dropping the elbow and then forwarding as Jum Sau, the left Jum Sau lifts at the elbow, rotates clockwise over the Dummy's arm, sticking at the wrist to form Kau Sau (*see* Fig 375).

Key points

- Do not clash with the Dummy's arm when applying Kau Sau or Jum Sau; stick to the Dummy at all times, applying either forward energy with Jum Sau or retracting energy with Kau Sau from contact.
- Look forward at the 'head' of the Dummy; do not look down.
- Use a short, sharp and powerful turning stance (Juen Ma) to increase the forward energy of Jum Sau and to create the retracting energy of Kau Sau.
- Maintain a good vertical posture, correct stance width and the necessary musculoskeletal structure in the arms.

Bong Sau to Tan Sau/Jic Gerk

Another fundamental drill of the fourth section is the Bong Sau to Tan Sau with a Jic Gerk to the side of the 'knee' of the Dummy's leg. This drill hones the ability to flow from Bong Sau to Tan Sau, whilst correctly positioning the body and transferring all the body's mass on to the one leg in order to deliver a powerful kick to the knee at 90 degrees to the Dummy.

Whilst rolling from Bong Sau to Tan Sau, maintain contact with the Dummy's arm and forward pressure into the Dummy throughout

Fig 373   Right Kau Sau/left
Jum Sau.

Fig 374   Roll half-way.

Fig 375   Jum Sau/Kau Sau
and repeat.

the movement. At the same time, Biu Ma step at approximately 45 degrees to the Dummy and turn the hips and shoulders parallel to the Dummy's leg, driving a front kick (Jic Gerk) to the side of the knee of the Dummy's leg at approximately 90 degrees to the Dummy's leg (*see* Fig 376). It is essential to ensure that the hip girdle is rotated forward, the back

Fig 376   Bong Sau/Wu Sau.

Fig 377   Tan Sau, Wan Jeung,
Jic Gerk.

Fig 378   Bong Sau/Wu Sau
and repeat.

139

straight and the weight centred over the heel of the supporting leg when applying Jic Gerk. The left arm can either form a Wu Sau or Wan Jeung (side palm) to the Dummy's body (*see* Fig 377). Drive the kicking leg down into a Biu Ma step, combined with a Bong Sau/Wu Sau to the opposite Dummy's arm (*see* Fig 378) and then continue to repeat the movements on to the other side of the Dummy.

Key points

- Do not disengage the Bong Sau and then clash with the Dummy's arm when applying Tan Sau; stick to and maintain contact with the Dummy's arm throughout the transition.
- Look forward at the 'head' of the Dummy; do not look down.
- Drive the Jic Gerk up and forwards from the floor into the Dummy's knee; strike using the centre of the heel.
- Maintain a good posture, tilting the hips slightly forward; keep a vertical posture with all the weight over the supporting leg when kicking.
- Resist the temptation to lean forward to ensure that the side palm makes contact.

Core Techniques of the Fifth Section

Po Pai Jeung

Drilling the Po Pai Jeung applications improves speed, reflexes and fluidity as well as the ability to apply energy into and control an opponent. The hand techniques utilize a variety of footwork – turning and stepping – both across the Dummy and around the leg, into the Dummy, and are especially useful for improving the ability to apply these movements powerfully within Chi Sau.

The drill can begin from a Bong Sau position (*see* Fig 379), rolling around the Dummy's arm, whilst stepping around and in with Po Pai Jeung (*see* Fig 380). As soon as both palms make light contact with the Dummy's body, apply a short, sharp push into the Dummy from the elbows, snapping the wrists forward and then immediately relaxing the hands and the fingers, and applying energy into, not on to, the Dummy. Step back around the Dummy's leg with Seung Gang Sau (*see* Fig 381) and then turn to face the Dummy, applying Po Pai Jeung (*see* Fig 382). Turn and apply Bong Sau (*see* Fig 383), and continue by rolling around the Dummy's arm, whilst stepping around and in with Po Pai Jeung (*see* Fig 384). Step back around the Dummy's leg with Kwun Sau (*see* Fig 385) and then turn to face the Dummy, again applying Po Pai Jeung (*see* Fig 386). Continue the drill by turning to Bong Sau again.

When applying the Bong Sau to Po Pai Jeung, it is important to practise two variations.

1. When rolling from Bong Sau, maintain contact at all times with the Dummy's arm, using the forearm and elbow of the upper Po Pai Jeung arm to stick to and control the Dummy's arm. The supporting Wu Sau becomes the lower Po Pai Jeung.
2. When rolling from Bong Sau, disengage the Bong Sau arm, dropping it into the lower Po Pai Jeung structure. The supporting Wu Sau drives forward to apply the upper Po Pai Jeung.

Key points

- Do not clash too forcefully with the Dummy's arm when applying Seung Gang Sau or Kwun Sau; stick to the Dummy whenever possible, applying

Fig 379   Bong Sau/Wu Sau.

Fig 380   Step around and in Po Pai Jeung.

Fig 381   Step back Seung Gang Sau at approximately 45 degrees.

Fig 382   Face with Po Pai Jeung.

Fig 383   Juen Ma, Bong Sau/Wu Sau.

Fig 384   Step around and in Po Pai Jeung.

forward energy into the Dummy as soon as contact is made.

- Make light contact with the fingers before applying Po Pai Jeung, driving energy into the Dummy's body.

- Look forward at the 'head' of the Dummy; do not look down.

- Use a short, sharp and powerful stepping (Biu Ma) and circling stance (Huen Ma) to move to the optimum

141

Left: Fig 385   Step back Kwun Sau.
Right: Fig 386   Face with Po Pai Jeung and repeat.

position to apply a powerful Po Pai Jeung.

- Maintain a good vertical posture, correct stance width and the necessary musculoskeletal structure in the arms.

Core Techniques of the Sixth Section

Bong Chor Sau, Lap Sau/Fak Da

As discussed earlier, the Bong Chor Sau, Lap Sau/Fak Da sequence can feel quite an awkward movement, and the resulting Lap Sau position does not necessarily feel comfortable. This is because in application the Lap Sau would pull, deflect and reposition the attacker's arm; on the Dummy, however, the arm cannot move and so the Lap Sau can feel a little cramped if incorrectly positioned. The key is to drill the sequence to develop a smooth and powerful transition from Bong Chor Sau, through to the Lap Sau position, apply the necessary Lap Sau energy and simultaneously deliver a powerful Fak Da strike (though not actually striking

the Dummy's body hard to avoid injuring the hand).

From a Bong Sau (*see* Fig 387) position turn (Juen Ma), rolling the Bong Sau to a Lap Sau, whilst maintaining contact with the Dummy's arm; at the same time the Wu Sau changes structure to become a Fak Sau strike (*see* Fig 388). The turn should be completed just as the Lap Sau energy is applied and the Fak Da makes contact with the Dummy's body. Immediately turn to face the Dummy in a neutral stance with a left Gum Sau and a right Wan Jeung palm strike (*see* Fig 389). The drill continues with the Gum Sau becoming a Bong Sau to the opposite Dummy's arm, supported by a Wu Sau in conjunction with a Juen Ma turning stance (*see* Fig 390).

Key points

- Do not clash with the Dummy's arm when applying Bong Sau.
- Stick to the Dummy; do not disengage contact when converting Bong Chor Sau into Lap Sau, applying forward energy into the Dummy until the Lap Sau is applied.

CLOCKWISE FROM TOP LEFT:
Fig 387   Juen Ma, Bong Sau/Wu Sau.
Fig 388   Juen Ma, Lap Sau/Fak Da.
Fig 389   Turn to face the Dummy, Gum Sau/Wan Jeung.
Fig 390   Juen Ma, Bong Sau/Wu Sau and repeat.

- Look forward at the 'head' of the Dummy; do not look down.
- Use a sharp and powerful turn (Juen Ma) to move to the optimum position to apply a powerful Lap Sau/Fak Sau combination and again to apply the Gum Sau/Wan Jeung combination.
- Maintain a good vertical posture, correct stance width and the necessary musculoskeletal structure in the arms.

Bong Sau to Tan Sau/Wan Jeung/Chut Sun Gerk

The second core technique of the sixth section of the Dummy is the Bong Sau to Tan Sau/Wu Sau/Chut Sun Gerk movement, applied whilst stepping around the Dummy's leg and repositioning at approximately 45 degrees.

The footwork in this sequence is unique and quite different to the other sections.

CLOCKWISE FROM TOP LEFT:
Fig 391   Bong Sau to left Dummy arm.
Fig 392   Tan Sau, half move on Dummy, feet together.
Fig 393   Tan Sau/Wu Sau, Chut Sun Gerk.
Fig 394   Tan/Wan Jeung, foot back on floor.
Fig 395   Biu Ma Bong Sau to right Dummy arm and repeat.

It involves kicks where the body's mass is transferred to the leg furthest from the Dummy, in preparation to kick with the leg nearest to the Dummy. In this instance, the body's mass is kept over the heel of the leg closest to the Dummy in order to kick with the other leg. Furthermore, the feet are momentarily brought side by side (*see* Fig 392), whilst pivoting on the heels to face the centre of the Dummy. Only then

can the cross-stamp kick (Chut Sun Gerk) be driven diagonally upwards and forwards from the supporting leg on to and into the Dummy's body.

The drill can commence from a Juen Ma Bong Sau position (*see* Fig 391). Step, reposition and re-angle the body as the Bong Sau flows smoothly into the Tan Sau, pressing forward from the elbow into the Dummy's body throughout the movement (*see* Fig 392).

The Wu Sau can either be maintained as a guard hand, illustrated in the photographs, or it can be driven forwards as a mid-level palm strike (Wan Jeung) to the Dummy's body, as previously discussed in the description of the sixth section of the Dummy form (*see* Fig 230).

The Chut Sun Jic Gerk should land simultaneously with the forming of the Tan Sau (*see* Fig 393) and, if deployed, the applying of the Wan Jeung palm strike. As soon as the kick has landed on the Dummy and the energy driven into the Dummy, the kicking leg should be quickly and powerfully placed back on the ground, alongside the supporting leg/foot (*see* Fig 394). In conjunction with a Biu Ma step, a Bong Sau/Wu Sau combination (*see* Fig 395) should then be applied to the opposite Dummy's arm in order to continue the drill.

When moving to the opposite side of the Dummy, the Bong Sau should roll over the Dummy's arm and then forward until the Bong Sau makes light contact with the last few inches of the Dummy's arm. The Bong Sau then applies a continuous pressure forwards via the contact point on the Dummy's arm, into the centre of the Dummy and then smoothly flows into the Tan Sau/Wu Sau/ Chut Sun Jic Gerk as discussed above.

Key points

- Maintain a forwarding energy from the elbow, through the wrist into the centre of the Dummy upon contact when applying the Bong Sau on to the Dummy's arm.
- Apply a short, sharp forwarding energy from the elbow, through the wrist into the centre of the Dummy upon contact when applying the Wan Jeung on to the Dummy's body, relaxing immediately afterwards.
- Do not clash with the Dummy's arm when applying Bong Sau or Wan Jeung;

make light contact and then apply forward energy.
- Stick to the Dummy's arm whilst rolling from Bong Sau to Tan Sau.
- Look forward at the 'head' of the Dummy; do not look at your feet.
- Drive the kick from the heel of the supporting leg forwards and upwards.
- Apply the Chut Sun Jic Gerk strike using the centre of the heel of the foot.
- Maintain a good vertical posture, correct stance width and the necessary musculoskeletal structure in the arms.

Core Techniques of the Seventh Section

Jic Gerk to Wan Gerk

Without continuous practice, the process of driving Jic Gerk up the centreline, followed immediately by a Wan Gerk side-stamp kick to the Dummy knee, can feel an awkward movement and one that does not flow easily. This is partly due to the use of the Tan Sau on the opposite side of the body to the Jic Gerk plus the requirement to maintain the body mass over the supporting leg, whilst pivoting around the centre of the heel to apply the Wan Gerk. The key is to drill the sequence sufficiently to develop a smooth and powerful transition from Jic Gerk to the Wan Gerk.

From a By Jong position (*see* Fig 396) in a neutral stance facing the Dummy, first bring what is to be the supporting leg into the centreline, directly in front of the Dummy. Then bring the kicking leg in front of the supporting leg and drive the Jic Gerk forwards and upwards to the Dummy's body, landing half-way between the leg and the low, middle arm. Simultaneously, drive the Tan Sau (using the arm on the opposite side of the body to the kick) forward to connect with the Dummy's arm and form a Wu Sau

with the rear hand. The Tan Sau and the Jic Gerk should make contact with the Dummy at the same time (*see* Fig 397). From the Jic Gerk position pivot on the heel of the supporting leg, angling the hips to approximately 45 degrees, leaning back slightly and applying a right Wan Gerk (stamping side-kick) on to the 'kneecap' of the Dummy's leg. Whilst angling the body to apply the Wan Gerk, rotate the right arm anticlock-wise from the Wu Sau position, lifting the elbow and forwarding the forearm to form a Bong Sau (*see* Fig 398). At the same time, retract the Tan Sau below the forming Bong Sau and forward as a Wu Sau to support the Bong Sau. As soon as the Wan Gerk strikes the Dummy, turn the hips and body to face the Dummy, placing the kicking leg back on the ground in a neutral stance. As the Wu Sau travels forward, the form By Jong and

CLOCKWISE FROM TOP LEFT:
Fig 400   Turn, Gum Sau/ Wu Sau.
Fig 401   Step approximately 45 degrees, Huen Ma, Wan Jeung, Wu Sau.
Fig 402   Stamp Huen Ma, Wan Jeung, Pak Sau.
Fig 403   Step back, Biu Ma, Gum Sau/Wu Sau and repeat.

the Bong Sau retracts beneath to form Wu Sau (*see* Fig 399).

Key points

- Correctly position the supporting leg on the centreline before attempting to apply the Jic Gerk.
- Maintain a good vertical posture, correct stance width and the necessary musculoskeletal structure in the arms when applying Jic Gerk.
- Maintain a good posture, leaning back slightly with all the weight over the supporting leg when applying Wan Gerk.
- When applying Wan Gerk, make light contact on the Dummy's body with the toes, and then apply a short, sharp stamp through the heel.

147

- Do not over-rotate the knee and hip when applying Wan Gerk; lift the kick at the knee and angle the knee and foot to a maximum of 45 degrees.
- Always look forward at the 'head' of the Dummy; do not look down.
- Use a sharp and powerful turn (Juen Ma) to move to the optimum position to apply a powerful Wan Gerk/Bong Sau, Wu Sau combination.

Gum Sau to Huen Ma

The purpose of this drill is to bring a familiarity to the Huen Ma application and instil an awareness of the body proximity and foot positions required to make the Huen Ma application easily available.

The drill begins from a Juen Ma/Gum Sau, Wu Sau position (*see* Fig 400). Step approximately 45 degrees and circle (Huen Ma) the leg around and then 'under' the Dummy's leg, placing the ball of the foot firmly on the floor beneath the Dummy's leg, whilst maintaining contact with the calf on to the underside of the Dummy's leg (*see* Fig 401). Then sharply straighten the leg, whilst simultaneously applying a Pak Sau cover to the nearest upper Dummy arm and applying a mid-level side palm (Wan Jeung) to the body of the Dummy (*see* Fig 402). Step around the leg and Biu Ma, forming a Gum Sau/Wu Sau to the low, middle Dummy arm (*see* Fig 403), then repeat as above.

Key points

- Correctly position the supporting leg before attempting to apply the Huen Ma.
- Maintain a good vertical posture, correct stance width and the necessary musculoskeletal structure in the arms when applying Huen Ma.

- When applying Huen Ma, make light contact on the Dummy's leg with the calf muscle; the foot must be positioned beneath the Dummy's leg, with a firm grip on the floor through the ball of the foot.
- Simultaneously, straighten the Huen Ma leg with a sharp and powerful 'stamp', whilst applying a mid-level Wan Jeung to the Dummy's body.
- Always look forward at the 'head' of the Dummy; do not look down.
- Check the feet are parallel to the Dummy after stepping around the Dummy's leg and before applying the stamp action to 'break' the opponent's stance.

Core Techniques of the Eighth Section

Dai Bong Sau, Tan Sau, Wan Jeung

This drill is designed to reinforce the principle that under certain (extreme) situations the same hand can be used to receive, protect and strike as opposed to always relying upon the simultaneous attack and defence approach. It can begin with a 45-degree Juen Ma, whilst driving a Dai Bong Sau forward on to the outside of the low, middle Dummy arm and covering the throat with a Wu Sau (*see* Fig 404). Immediately turn to face the Dummy in a neutral stance, rolling the Dai Bong Sau up and forward as a Tan Sau to the inside of the upper Dummy's arm (*see* Fig 405). From the Tan Sau, drive the arm forward on to the Dummy to 'strike' as Wan Jeung (*see* Fig 406), remaining relaxed and then snapping energy forward and into the Dummy upon contact. Drop the Wan Jeung down the centreline to form Dai Bong Sau on to the outside of the low, middle arm whilst turning at 45 degrees, and repeat the movements on the other side of the Dummy.

CLOCKWISE FROM TOP LEFT:
Fig 404   Turn 45 degrees,
Dai Bong/Wu Sau.
Fig 405   Face the Dummy,
Tan Sau/Wu Sau.
Fig 406   Wan Jeung/Wu
Sau.
Fig 407   Turn 45 degrees,
Dai Bong/Wu Sau and
repeat.

Key points

- Maintain a forwarding energy from the elbow, through the wrist into the centre of the Dummy upon contact when applying the Dai Bong Sau on to the Dummy's arm.
- Maintain a forwarding energy from the elbow, through the wrist into the centre of the Dummy upon contact when applying the Tan Sau and the Wan Jeung on to the Dummy's body.
- Do not clash with the Dummy's arm when applying Bong Sau, Tan Sau or Wan Jeung; make light contact, and then apply forward energy.
- Look forward at the 'head' of the Dummy; do not look down.

Fig 408   Gum Sau/Wu Sau.   Fig 409   Pak Sau/Wu Sau, Jic   Fig 410   Gum Sau/Wu Sau
                               Gerk.   and repeat.

- Maintain a good vertical posture, correct stance width and the necessary musculoskeletal structure in the arms.

Gum Sau to Pak Sau/ Wu Sau with Jic Gerk

Another fundamental drill of the eighth section is the Gum Sau to Pak Sau/Wu Sau with a Jic Gerk applied to the 'knee' of the Dummy's leg. This drill hones the ability to flow from a low Gum Sau to a high Pak Sau, whilst correctly turning and positioning the body, transferring all the body's mass on to the supporting leg in order to deliver a powerful short-range kick to the knee at 45 degrees to the Dummy.

From a Gum Sau (*see* Fig 408) on to the low Dummy arm (with a Wu Sau cover), take a small Biu Ma step parallel to the Dummy, and then turn sharply, transferring the body's mass on to the supporting leg, driving forward a Pak Sau to the outside of the upper Dummy arm and a Jic Gerk to the knee of the Dummy's leg (*see* Fig 409). Put the kick

down to the floor as a Biu Ma step and form a low Gum Sau (with a Wu Sau cover) to the outside of the low Dummy arm and continue the drill (*see* Fig 410).

Key points

- Do not clash with the Dummy's arm when applying Pak Sau; apply a short, sharp wrist-snap energy into the Dummy's arm, towards the Dummy and then immediately relax, leaving the palm in contact with the Dummy's arm.
- Look forward at the 'head' of the Dummy; do not look down.
- Drive the Jic Gerk up and forwards from the floor into the Dummy's knee; strike using the centre of the heel.
- Maintain a good vertical posture, tilting the hips forward slightly, keeping a vertical posture with all the weight over the supporting leg when kicking.
- Always kick directly away from the supporting leg.

Fig 411   Juen Ma, Bong Sau/ Wu Sau.

Fig 412   Juen Ma, Seung Lap Sau/Pak Gerk.

Fig 413   Juen Ma, Bong Sau/ Wu Sau and repeat.

Bong Chor Sau to Seung Lap Sau with Pak Gerk

The final drill of the eighth section and of the entire Dummy form is the Bong Chor Sau to Seung Lap Sau with Pak Gerk. The aim of this drill is to develop a fast, smooth transition from the Bong Chor Sau to the Seung Lap Sau, which in effect disguises the application of the Pak Gerk until the effect of the kick is felt on the shin or the front of the ankle.

From a Bong Chor Sau position in a 45-degree turned stance (*see* Fig 411), turn sharply, converting the Bong Chor Sau to Lap Sau (using Jut Sau energy) to control the attacker's wrist, whilst driving the rear Wu Sau forward to contact and control the attacker's elbow joint (*see* Fig 412). At the same time, apply a sharp Pak Gerk with the heel of the foot on to the 'shin' of the Dummy. Take a short, sharp step (Biu Ma) as the foot is placed back on the floor, applying a Bong Chor Sau to the other upper arm of the Dummy and repeat the above movement.

Key points

- Do not clash with the Dummy's arm when applying Bong Sau.
- Stick to the Dummy; do not disengage contact when converting Bong Chor Sau into Lap Sau, applying forward energy into the Dummy until the Lap Sau is applied.
- Look forward at the 'head' of the Dummy; do not look down.
- Use a sharp and powerful turn (Juen Ma) to move to the optimum position to apply a powerful Lap Sau/Pak Gerk combination.
- Maintain a good vertical posture, correct stance width and the necessary musculoskeletal structure in the arms.

Free Application

As discussed earlier, the third and final stage of practising on the Dummy is to apply the techniques within each section in any logical

151

sequence in order to free the practitioner of the restraints of the form. The objective is to flow smoothly and logically from technique to technique without adherence or reference to the sequence of the form, utilizing all of Wing Chun's tools and principles in a spontaneous, yet controlled and logical flow on what is, in essence, a three-dimensional static opponent. Whilst free flowing on the Dummy, the Wing Chun practitioner should mentally treat and visualize the Dummy as if it were a real opponent, sticking and controlling the limbs and the leg, forwarding energy into the Dummy directly or via the limbs, and making each movement and position tight, powerful and fast. The Wing Chun practitioner should constantly check his posture, position and structure to ensure they are correct, whilst refining their timing so that the correct combination of hand techniques, kicks and stance-work arrive simultaneously and powerfully.

Three Phases to Learning to Apply the Wooden Dummy Techniques

In addition to the three key stages to learning the Dummy form discussed in detail above, and in keeping with the significance of the number three, considered lucky in Chinese culture, there are three phases to learning and refining the Wooden Dummy techniques for use in combat application.

First Phase

Having learnt, practised and refined the movements of the form, drilled the primary and secondary core techniques and freely applied the Dummy techniques as discussed above, the Wing Chun practitioner should train each technique in the sections to develop the correct structure, position, footwork and energy. This involves drilling each technique (rather than sequence) from each section on the Dummy individually – Juen Ma, Tan Da, and so on. The purpose of this method of drilling, as opposed to those in Mor Jong (*see above*), is to drill the application of the techniques for application on a partner or opponent.

Second Phase

The Dummy techniques should then be practised with, and applied on, a partner to develop and refine them as a combat application.

The primary objective of applying the techniques on a partner is to develop the ability to extract the sterile, 'perfect' shapes, structures and body positions developed on the fixed structure of the Dummy, adjust, and adapt them for use on a real person. They can be practised and applied as a combination/sequence in a self-defence scenario to practise real-world/real-time application, or in isolation as a drill to develop improved timing, structure and positions. Additionally, they can be worked into Chi Sau practice to improve the timing, sensitivity and reflexes of close-quarter attack and defence applications.

Third Phase

The final phase, *Dar Hung Jong*, is practice of the form without the Dummy to develop fluidity, coordination and balance. This entails performing the entire Wooden Dummy form without the aid of the Dummy to check the accuracy of positions, structure and posture without the framework of the Dummy for reference. It is not difficult to develop and maintain 'perfect' positioning, structures, footwork and kicks when you have a Dummy to contact and 'check' the shapes. It is considerably more difficult to do the same without the Dummy, and takes a much greater understanding and appreciation of the moves and shapes plus a higher degree of muscle control to position the body and the limbs correctly and hold them there.

4 Conclusion

Over the years many variations of the Dummy form have developed. However, this book is written with the aim of cataloguing and describing the Dummy form as Sifu Ip Chun taught it to me during my first few trips to Hong Kong. Furthermore, it is my intention that this book be used as a reference tool for Wing Chun instructors and students alike; it was not written as a teaching manual because it is not possible to learn Wing Chun from a book.

I hope that all who read this book have the open-mindedness and flexibility of thought to accept that although there may be variations of the form, commonalities can be embraced.

In closing, I would like to reiterate that without the aid of a competent instructor, learning the intricate details of the Wooden Dummy form and the drills associated with it is an impossible task.

Author's Notes

Jut Sau/Tok Sau
Some Wing Chun Sifus teach a Jut Sau/Tok Sau movement between the eight sections to 'punctuate' the sections. These movements are not included in the 116 movements of the Dummy form and may be either included or excluded. I was not taught the Jut Sau/Tok Sau movements and so do not teach or include it.

I was once told that these movements originally stemmed from Grandmaster Ip Man, not for any practical or aesthetic purpose, but because the vertical supports on Ip Man's Dummy were positioned far apart and the horizontal struts quite springy. After the Jut Sau/Jic Jeung movement at the end of each section, the Dummy would continue to 'rock', causing the upper arms to shake loose and move forward. Apparently, Ip Man would use Seung Jut Sau to stop it rocking and then Seung Tok Sau to 'push' the upper arms back into the Dummy.

Additional Gum Sau Movements
Around 1992, Sifu Ip Chun included an additional Gum Sau movement before the Huen Ma movement in the seventh section, and again before the Pak Sau/Wu Sau, Jic Gerk movement in the eighth section. How, when and where these movements originated I do not know; however, I can vividly recall when I first became aware of their existence.

In April 1992 I hosted a seminar for both Sifu Ip Chun and his younger brother Ip Ching at my Birmingham school. The next day, while discussing the Dummy at my home, I witnessed an animated discussion and the two of them alternately demonstrating various sections of the Dummy regarding various movements and applications, including the inclusion or exclusion of the additional Gum Sau movements. Due to my limited grasp of Cantonese, I could not grasp the 'intricacies' of the conversation; I was still in awe of having both of Grandmaster Ip Man's sons at my home alternatively demonstrating and discussing various movements from the Dummy form after having already practised Chi Sau with both of them.

Suffice to say, I have not included the additional Gum Sau movements within the form in this book because I am not in the habit of including or teaching movements that I have not been taught.

Purchasing a Wooden Dummy

Purchasing a Wooden Dummy is a big decision for a Wing Chun practitioner since they can be expensive and require a lot of room, both to store and in order to train on it.

There are several fundamental decisions to be made: should the Dummy be a traditional one made of wood or a more modern alternative? Should it be a live Dummy on a frame, a 'dead' Dummy (a stake into the ground) or a freestanding one? The answers to these questions often depend upon where your Dummy will be located.

I have selected three examples that I believe worthy of serious consideration:

1. Traditional Wooden Dummy
   Pagoda Imports Wooden Dummy
   The Old Bakery, Lower Square
   Forest Row, East Sussex
   01342 824888
   info@WoodenDummies.co.uk

2. Freestanding Wooden Dummy
   The Traditional Wooden Dummy Company
   Mr Cameron Charles
   01280 701389
   07971 405582

3. Immortal Dense Resinous Polymer 'Wooden Dummy'
   Immortal Creations Ltd
   20 Doddington Road
   Chatteris
   Cambridgeshire PE16 6UA
   01354 696175
   sales@immortal.co.uk

OPPOSITE: Fig 414 An abbreviated Ip Man Wing Chun family tree.

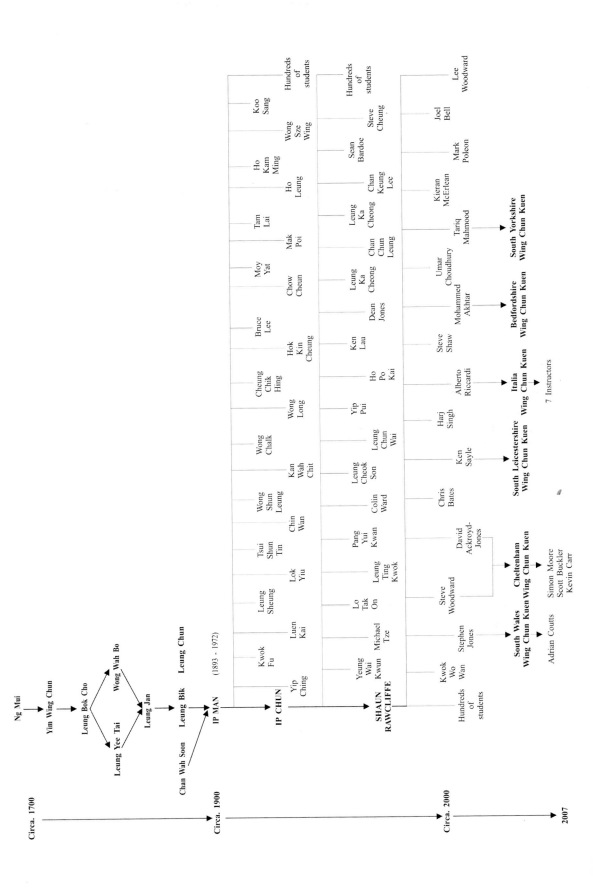

Wing Chun Maxims

General Sayings

- *Da sau jic siu sau* – The hand that hits, also blocks.
- *Kuen yau sum fot* – The punch comes from the heart.
- *Ying da juk da, but ying da, but hor da, mo keung da, mo luen da* – When you should hit, hit; when you shouldn't, don't; don't when you can't; don't when you mustn't.
- *Sau gerk sheung shui, mo juet jiu* – Hand against hand, foot against foot, there is no unstoppable technique.
- *Loy lau hui sung* – Hand comes, detain; hand goes, follow.
- *Lut sau jic chung* – Hand lost, thrust forward.
- *Jung shun doi yeng* – Face your opponent with your centreline.
- *Juck sun ye, bok wai ng* – When facing your opponent with your side, your shoulder becomes the centreline.
- *Siu se but lean kung, lo loy yat cheung hung* – If you do not train hard when you are young, you will have nothing when you are old.
- *Chor hock mo yung lic* – Beginners must not use strength.
- *Kuen mo lai yeung, quan mo leung heung* – When using fist, do not stand on ceremony, when using staff, do not expect two sounds.
- *Yan han gung, ngor han yin* – Whilst others walk the bow, I walk the string.
- *Lin siu dai da* – Simultaneous attack and defence.
- *Bong Chor Sau hai gerk* – Wrong Bong Sau, use kick.
- *Pak sau ge noi mun* – Pak Sau avoids the inner gate.
- *Yung Gerk Jang Wu dui* – Whenever kicking the heels face each other.

- *Kwun Sau po pai Jeung* – After Kwun Sau, follow Po Pai Jeung.
- *Chi Sau leung bye muk* – Chi Sau with both eyes closed.

'Yee' Gee Kim Yeung Ma Maxims

- Pull in the chest, push out the upper back, and bring in the tailbone.
- Fill the Dan Tien with Ch'i and distribute throughout the body.
- Point the knees and toes inwards.
- Form a pyramid with the centre of gravity in the middle.
- Fists are placed at the sides, but not resting against the body.
- Sink the elbows, the shoulders and the waist.
- Hold the head and neck straight and keep the spirit alert.
- Eyes are level, looking forward and aware of all directions.
- The mind is free of distractions and the mood is positive.
- There is no fear when facing the opponent.
- Yee Gee Kim Yeung Ma is the main training stance.
- Develop a good foundation for advanced techniques.

Siu Nim Tao Maxims

小念頭

- Siu Nim Tao comes first; do not force progress in training.
- A weak body must start with strength improvement.
- Do not retain bad habits.

156

- Yee Gee Kim Yeung Ma – trains the Ch'i by controlling the Dan Tien.
- To maintain good balance and strength, grip the ground with the toes.
- To release Ch'i from the Dan Tien will enable proper release of energy.
- Sink the elbows and relax the shoulders, guarding the centreline to protect both sides.
- There are one hundred and eight moves, all practical and real.
- Thousands of variations can be used, aiming for practical use and not beauty.
- Internally develop the Ch'i; externally train the tendons, bones and muscles.
- Tan Sau, Bong Sau, Fook Sau, Wu Sau and Huen Sau; their wonder grows with practice.
- Each movement must be crisp and precise. Timing is essential.
- Practise once a day; more will cause no harm.

Chum Kiu Maxims

尋橋

- Chum Kiu trains the stance and the waist; the arm bridge is short and the step is narrow.
- Eyes are trained to be alert; the Ch'i flows in a perpetual motion.
- Strive to remain calm in the midst of motion; loosen up the muscles and relax the mind.
- Turning the stance with a circular movement will allow superior generation of power.
- When the opponent's arm bridge enters the arm bridge, use the escaping hand to turn around the situation.
- Pass by the opponent's incoming arm bridge from above, without stopping when the countering move has started.

- Lan Sau and Jip Sau put an opponent in danger.
- Do not collide with a strong opponent; with a weak opponent use a direct frontal assault.
- A quick fight should be ended quickly; no delay is allowed.
- Use the three joints of the arm to prevent entry by the opponent's bridge; jam the opponent's bridge to restrict his movement.
- Create a bridge if the opponent's bridge is not present; nullify the bridge according to how it is presented.
- The arm bridge tracks the movement of the opponent's body; when the hands cannot prevail, use body position to save the situation.
- Using short-range power to jam the opponent's bridge, the three joints are nicely controlled.
- Where is the opponent's bridge to be found? Chum Kiu guides the way.

Biu Tze Maxims

標指

- Biu Tze contains emergency techniques.
- Iron fingers can strike a vital point at once.
- Close-range elbow strikes have sufficient threatening power.
- The Phoenix eye punch has no compassion.
- Fak Sau, Ginger punch and Guide bridge; their movements are closely coordinated and hard to defend and nullify.
- Springy power and the extended arm are applied at close range.
- The situation is different when preventing defeat in an emergency.
- Biu Tze is not taught outside the family.
- How many Sifus pass on the proper heritage?

Glossary

Wing Chun – Cantonese name for practical southern Chinese martial art

Kuen – Fist, a hand with the fingers clenched into the palm

Siu Nim Tao – Little idea method; way of the small idea

Chum Kiu – Seeking the bridge

Biu Tze – Thrusting fingers

Chi Sau – Sticking hands

Muk Yan Jong – Wooden Dummy

Baat Cham Dao – Eight chopping knives; butterfly knives

Luk Dim Boon Kwun – Six-and-a-half-point pole

Biu Ma – Thrusting forward stance

Biu Sau – Thrusting arm

Biu Tze Sau – Thrusting fingers

Bong Sau – Wing arm

By Jong – Ready stance

Chair Pie – Diagonal elbow strike

Chang Sau – Cutting hand; spade hand

Chao Kuen – Whipping hand; rising punch

Chi Sau Lye Bye Muk – Both eyes closed; blindfold Chi Sau

Chun Ging – Inch energy; one-inch punch

Chung Sum Seen – Central heart line

Cup Jarn – Vertical elbow strike

Chut Sun Jic Gerk – Opposite (cross-stamp) kick

Da – Hit or strike

Dai Bong Sau – Low wing arm

Dan Chi Sau – Single sticking hands

Dar Hung Jong – Practising the Dummy, without a Dummy

Ding Sau/Jeung – High bridging hand/strike

Dok Sau – Exploration; think-tank (within Chi Sau)

Dung Toi – Lifting kick

Fa Ging – Release energy

Fak Sau – Whisking hand

Fook Sau – Controlling/bridging hand

Fut Sau – Flicking hands

Gang Sau – Splitting arm

Gor Sau – Free application

Gerk Fa – Kicking techniques

Gum Sau – Pinning hand

Gung Lik – Energy that hard work and effort produces over a long period of training

Gwoy Jarn – Horizontal elbow strike

Huen Sau – Circling hand

Huen Ma – Circling stance

Jeung Sau – Changing arms

Jic Gerk – Front kick

Jic Jeung – Vertical/straight palm

Jic Seen – Centreline; straight line

Jip Sau – Folding arms

Juen Ma – Turning stance

Jum Sau – Sinking arm

Jut Sau – Jerking hand

Kau Sau – Scooping hand

Kei Gi – Real fighting

Kuen Tou – Hand forms

Kwun Sau – Rotating arms

Lan Sau – Bar arm

Lap Sau – Deflecting hand

Lin Wan Kuen – Chain punches; consecutive punch

Man Geng Sau – Neck pulling hand

Mor Jong – Polishing the Dummy (drilling exercises on the Dummy)

Mun Sau – Asking hand

Noy Mun – Inside gate

Oi Mun – Outside gate
Pai Jarn – Hacking elbows
Pak Gerk – Slapping kick
Pak Sau – Clapping/slapping hand
Po Pai Jeung – Double pushing palms
Poon Sau – Rolling arms
Seung Chi Sau – Double sticking hands
Si Dai – Junior Kung Fu brother
Si Gung – Kung Fu Grandfather; teacher's teacher
Si Hing – Senior Kung Fu brother
Si Je – Elder Kung Fu sister
Si Mo – Sifu's wife
Si Mui – Junior Kung Fu sister
Sifu – Teacher; Kung Fu father

Sung Lik – Soft energy (withdrawing the force)
Tan Sau – Dispersing hand
Tek – Leg
To Dei – Student
Tse M Seen – Meridian line
Wan Gerk – Sidekick
Wan Jeung – Side palm
Wan Tan Gerk – 135-degree kick
Wu Sau – Protective hand
Yat Chi Kuen – Character 'sun' thrusting punch
Yee Gee Kim Yeung Ma – Basic training stance

References

Abernethy, P., Wilson, G. and Logan, P., Strength and power assessment: Issues, controversies and challenges, *Sports Medicine*, vol. 19, pp. 401–417 (1995)

Confucius, *The Doctrine of the Mean* (Zhong Yong Chung Yung). Trans. Chan, W. T., *A Sourcebook in Chinese Philosophy*, (Princeton, NJ: Princeton University Press, 1963)

HarperCollins, *Collins Pocket English Dictionary* (Glasgow, 1996)

Hislop, H. J. and Perrine, J. J., The isokinetic concept of exercise. *Journal of the American Physical Therapy Association*, vol. 447, pp. 114–117 (1967)

Jackson, S. M. and Bemmet, P. J., *Physiology with Anatomy for Nurses* (Baillière Tindall, 1988)

Kwok, M.-H., Palmer, M. and Ramsay, J. *Tao Te Ching* (Shaftesbury, Dorset: Element, 1993)

Moy, Y. and Kwong, C. N., *Ving Tsun Kuen Kuit* (Tallahassee, 1982)

Newton, I., *The Principia: Mathematical Principles of Natural Philosophy*, trans. Cohen, I. B. and Whitman, A. (Berkeley, CA: University of California, 1999)

Race, P., *The Lecturer's Toolkit – A Practical Guide to Assessment, Learning and Teaching* (Routledge, Oxon, 2007)

Tzu, S., *The Art of War* (various)

Index